BUSES
YEARBOOK 2007

Edited by STEWART J. BROWN

Ian Allan
PUBLISHING

BUSES
YEARBOOK 2007

Contents

First published 2006

ISBN (10) 0 7110 3116 9
ISBN (13) 978 0 7110 3116 6

© Ian Allan Publishing Ltd 2006

Published by Ian Allan Publishing

an imprint of Ian Allan Publishing Ltd,
Hersham, Surrey KT12 4RG.
Printed in England by Ian Allan Printing Ltd,
Hersham, Surrey KT12 4RG.

Code: 0608/E3

Visit the Ian Allan Publishing website at
www.ianallanpublishing.com

Front cover:
The advent of minibuses was one
of the most significant
developments of the 1980s. This
Mercedes-Benz L608D belonged to
Brighton & Hove, carved out of
Southdown in 1986. *Gavin Booth*

Back cover (upper):
Instead of deregulation, London's
buses became subject to tendering
and privatisation. Even so, the
traditional Routemasters continued
in service until the end of 2005,
with many refurbished. *Gavin Booth*

Back cover (lower):
The future, or 'ftr', belongs to
FirstGroup's Volvo B7LA/Wright
Streetcar artics, which made their
debut in York in May 2006.
Gavin Booth

Title page:
Blazefield subsidiary Yorkshire
Coastliner introduced Eclipse
Geminis on inter-urban services.
One loads in York on its way to
Leeds. *Stewart J. Brown*

The Year of Takeovers

A rash of takeovers in 2005 and early 2006 has redrawn the map of British bus ownership. *Buses* editor ALAN MILLAR investigates.

The word 'consolidation' was one we heard a lot in the 1990s. It was how commentators termed what was happening to the newly privatised British bus industry, as management and, in a few cases, management/employee teams cashed in on their initial investments and allowed their companies to be absorbed into the Big Five groups that were emerging as the new force in bus operation.

By 2000, when Arriva acquired MTL North, there wasn't a lot left to consolidate that hadn't already been consolidated. Besides that, the groups had begun to spread their acquisitive wings overseas. Stagecoach, First and National Express were buying up companies in North America, while Arriva was moving steadily into mainland Europe, and all were keen to expand their involvement in running British trains. There also were suggestions that the big groups' day had passed and that the future belonged to medium-sized regional businesses willing to pick up the less attractive parts of the Big Five's routes and earn healthy returns from them. Not only that, but most of the remaining mini-groups and management buy-outs retained their independence because they wanted to. Many could, no doubt, have sold their companies for more millions than they would have dreamed of 20 years earlier and sailed off into the sunset to enjoy untold numbers of rounds of golf and luxury cruises. But these guys still enjoyed running their businesses and were in no rush — yet — to accept the big groups' millions.

If those were the trends of the first years of the third millennium, they ended in 2005 and the first weeks of 2006 as a new round of consolidation left only three of the 55 regional bus and coach companies sold by the National Bus Company in the years 1986-8 still in independent ownership. For the record, those survivors are Trent Barton, East Yorkshire and Ambassador Travel. NBC had created Great Yarmouth-based Ambassador in 1984, when it split Eastern Counties in three. Just as endangered a species was the traditional municipal, only 16 still being in council ownership (two of them with minority private-sector shareholdings) and one ex-municipal — Preston Bus — remaining in employee ownership.

So why the sudden rush of takeovers? Probably a combination of factors. Some of the owners of the privatised companies had reached (or soon would reach) retirement age, and as these were not family businesses in the traditional sense their sons and daughters were unlikely to take over the reins. Nor, for that matter, were the sons and daughters of several family-owned independents that sold up at the same time.

Spiralling operating costs no doubt played a part too. World oil prices rocketed through much of 2005, and with economists pointing to Chinese industrialisation, continuing Middle East instability and dwindling stocks in the North Sea, there seems every chance that fuel costs will continue rising. Small-to-medium-sized operators are less able than the big groups to absorb these cost shocks. The same can be said of rising labour and insurance costs and of the general burden of red tape.

Then there is the perception that the bus entrepreneurs' best years are behind them. Traffic congestion and car ownership are rising, adding further to bus operators' costs and undermining their ability to compete against the private car. And in the big cities (outside London) the passenger transport executives and their political masters have been lobbying ever harder to regain control of bus services.

If this cocktail of reasons to sell were not enough, the big groups were also beginning to show renewed interest in UK bus operations. Stagecoach, a darling of the City which seemingly could do no wrong in the 1990s, got its fingers badly burnt overseas, especially in North America. After a period licking its wounds, selling its least successful overseas acquisitions and refocusing its UK bus businesses it was once again ready to buy bus companies at home. National Express ended 2005 having moved into Spain big-time, but it also pulled out of Australia, sold part of its North American business and seized an opportunity to expand in England.

As the new year dawned, clues of the changing tide were washing up on various industry shorelines. One was the painfully protracted demise of 2 Travel Grou

This Swansea-based coach and contract-bus operator had floated on the Alternative Investment Market a couple of years earlier. It was run by a couple of ex-FirstGroup managers and had secured City investors' funds by promising to expand in South Wales and the Bristol area as it predicted that First and others would contract. Neither First nor 2 Travel did as expected, and the business made no significant acquisitions, running into vehicle-maintenance problems and out of money.

Less obvious at the time was that Tellings Golden Miller, which had followed 2 Travel with an AIM listing about six months later, wasn't fulfilling its dreams either. It had picked up two small London bus and coach businesses but entered 2005 having lost out to Metroline — part of Singapore-based ComfortDelGro — in the bidding to buy Armchair, one of the biggest independents still running buses for Transport for London. Quite simply, the bigger boys were prepared to pay more than TGM could afford when bus companies came up for sale.

The other obvious piece of flotsam was rolling up and down Bournemouth seafront, where the Liberal Democrat-controlled council had put Yellow Buses up for sale towards the end of 2004. This may not have been the most commercially sparkling of Britain's bus companies — it gave all the appearance of managing decline rather than chasing growth opportunities — but that didn't stop the big groups from running their slide rules over its books.

FirstGroup — with the two parts of its Hampshire & Dorset business running to the east and west of Bournemouth — is thought to have been interested in adding this urban operation, but the group that pursued its ambitions most publicly was Go-Ahead. It had already bought Wilts & Dorset, based in nearby Poole and already a significant operator in the area, as part policy of expanding into the parts of southern and where it believes there are real growth

opportunities for public transport.

Go-Ahead also had a new Chief Executive, Chris Moyes, previously the deputy and a career busman, having succeeded the more cautious Martin Ballinger. He had admitted in public — in the friendliest possible way — that he thought his predecessor should have pursued the opportunity that had arisen in 2001 for Go-Ahead to expand into Merseyside and buy Gillmoss depot, which Arriva had been ordered to sell. Ballinger had persuaded his colleagues to pull out of that deal at the eleventh hour.

The deal that Go-Ahead offered in Bournemouth was nothing short of consolidation. It would take over Yellow Buses, merge it with Wilts & Dorset and provide a single network of higher-frequency services, supported by rapid replacement of the less-than-youthful Yellow Buses fleet. In short, it would offer Bournemouth what it already provided in Brighton, where its existing Brighton & Hove subsidiary had taken over the former council bus company. Just to add to the pressure, it also expanded Wilts & Dorset's presence in Bournemouth with 'More'-branded high-frequency core routes.

The council, it appears, was more interested in securing the highest price for Yellow Buses. As the months unfolded it found a buyer, but before it was finally able to tie up that deal it was obliged to put the company back on the market. The buyer wasn't any of the Big Five but Transdev, the French public-transport group that already owned London United and London Sovereign and had an 18% shareholding in Nottingham City Transport. It paid an astonishing £15 million for Yellow Buses and, as events would prove, was eager to expand its UK bus interests in other areas.

Go-Ahead's South Coast expansion plans didn't hang solely on the Bournemouth opportunity. In May 2005 it agreed a £13.8 million deal to buy Southern ectis and its Solent Blue Line subsidiary, taking the group into greater Southampton and onto the Isle of Wight. By the end of the year both were being managed by the Wilts & Dorset team, albeit retaining their separate identities.

Go-Ahead maintains a less iron grip on its subsidiaries than most of the other big groups, but even so a group preference for Mercedes-Benz Citaros was apparent in an order for delivery in 2006 to Solent Blue Line, which also took some of Oxford Bus Company's Volvo B10Bs off its hands.

At the same time as the Southern Vectis takeover was agreed the Brighton & Hove company struck another deal to take over Stagecoach's Lewes operations, in September 2005. Go-Ahead took over 20 vehicles' worth of routes along with 15 actual Stagecoach buses — but not the depot, which was

closed for redevelopment. It continued a pattern set in 2001, when Stagecoach had sold its under-performing East Lancashire operations to Blazefield, and Go-Ahead's Metrobus subsidiary had taken over Arriva's services in Crawley.

Go-Ahead's hunger for growth led to the £2 million takeover in December of the Birmingham Coach Company, a business with 123 vehicles — buses on commercial urban services in the West Midlands and coaches on National Express contracts. It's worth noting that the fleet is about the same size as Bournemouth's Yellow Buses, but the sale price was less than a seventh of what Transdev paid. Besides being an opportunity for Go-Ahead to run commercial services in competition with National Express-owned Travel West Midlands, it also provides the group with a means of bidding for franchised services should the

Left: Southern Vectis is now part of Go-Ahead Group. Purchased shortly before the change of ownership was a batch of Mini Pointer Darts from Alexander Dennis.
Mark Lyons

Right: The Birmingham Coach Company was bought by Go-Ahead at the end of 2005. Its fleet included this Optare Excel which had previously been operated by Metrobus — coincidentally also owned by Go-Ahead.
Luke Gottard

PTEs — like Centro in the West Midlands — regain control over their bus networks.

The year's takeovers also helped emphasise the changing shape of Go-Ahead, for its expansion in the South of England and into the West Midlands contrasted with the continuing decline in its original business in the North East. In a complete reversal of the 2001 deal in Crawley it announced plans to close its Go North East company's Bishop Auckland depot in April 2006, selling most routes to Arriva, which already had a depot in the town.

Lewes was Stagecoach's only significant retreat in a year of big takeover deals. The process began modestly on 1 April 2005, when Stagecoach Manchester bought Dennis's of Dukinfield and kept most of its 31 relatively modern vehicles. Dennis's had been a thorn in Stagecoach's side for some time, competing on the busy Ashton–Manchester corridor. The company — Dennis was its founder's forename — had been around since 1946 and had started running local bus services in 1986. Significant as it was in a regional context, this acquisition was but a foretaste of the substantial territorial expansion that was to come. Three months later Stagecoach moved into Merseyside by purchasing the business Go-Ahead had pulled back from buying four years earlier. Glenvale Transport — formed by former MTL top managers — had taken over the Gillmoss operation from Arriva and had stepped up competition on several main corridors into Liverpool. It had doubled in size — to a fleet just short of 300 buses — by acquiring CMT Buses, then the largest independent left in the city, but had nowhere obvious to go next.

Glenvale had talked of an AIM listing and maybe a move into the London bus market, but with the possibility of the Liverpool–Kirkby tram line being built through part of Gillmoss and taking away a good slice of Glenvale's revenue, it was keen to sell. Two of the French groups involved in the ultimately doomed tram project were thought to be interested, but Stagecoach seized the moment with a £3.4 million cash deal that also saw it assume more than twice that sum in debt. This was a classic Stagecoach deal of the sort that had characterised the group's earlier years, taking it into a promising urban area in which it had no real presence before and allowing it to make an immediate impact by replacing an elderly fleet with new and mid-life buses that would cost less to maintain.

Glenvale hadn't bought a single new bus. Its newest vehicles were low-floor single-deckers inherited mainly from Arriva and CMT, and most of its purchases were of second-hand Leyland Titans and MCW Metrobuses from London and, latterly, large numbers of step-entrance Dennis Darts and Volvo B6s. Most of the Darts and B6s were entering their second lives with Stagecoach, having reached Glenvale via Ensignbus, the Essex dealer. By early 2006 much of the inherited fleet had been replaced by new and refurbished low-floor Darts (the refurbished buses having been damaged when Carlisle depot was flooded the previous winter) and Volvo B10M-55 buses.

The ink was barely dry on the Glenvale deal when Stagecoach announced another, in September. This was not a straight takeover but a joint venture that saw it buy a 35% shareholding in Scottish Citylink from ComfortDelGro. While its Singapore-based partner retained financial control, there was no doubt about who now wore the trousers. Stagecoach's Scottish

Left: The Glenvale business, bought by Stagecoach in 2005, operated an elderly fleet consisting mainly of Leyland Titans and Dennis Darts. The latter included some unusual Wright Handybus models which had been new to Go-Ahead Northern. *Stewart J. Brown*

Right: The Glenvale Titans would be short-lived, the last being withdrawn in the early months of 2006. They did, however, carry Stagecoach fleetnames, as seen here in Liverpool city centre. *Philip Halewood*

Below: Among the younger buses in the Glenvale fleet was this Volvo B10B/Alexander Strider which had been new to Blazefield subsidiary Harrogate & District. *Philip Halewood*

Right: The Citylink and Megabus names on the windscreen of this Stagecoach-owned Jonckheere-bodied Volvo B10M in Edinburgh reveal the new levels of co-operation between the former rivals after Stagecoach and Citylink owner ComfortDelGro set up a joint venture in 2005. *Philip Halewood*

managing director was in overall charge, and — perhaps more trivial, but significant nonetheless — most routes lost their Citylink numbers for M-prefixed nubers in Stagecoach's Megabus series. In many ways this marked the end of a 25-year battle. Stagecoach had started out as an express coach operator linking the main Scottish cities, and the Scottish Bus Group had set up Citylink to respond to that challenge. And although there had been several comings and goings over the years — and Citylink changed hands a few times — the battles intensified during 2004, with Stagecoach launching Megabus and acquiring the Motorvator service between Edinburgh and Glasgow. The new joint venture killed off the Motorvator brand,

but Stagecoach subsidiaries took over several service from contracted operators.

The final deal of the year — announced in mid-December — was another classic Stagecoach one. It paid £26 million for Traction Group, the largest privately-owned bus group, and took on its £11 million debt. Traction was short for Yorkshire Traction, the original ex-NBC company in the group, whose other main subsidiaries were Road Car, in Lincolnshire and Nottinghamshire, and Strathtay, in Stagecoach's heartland to the east of Perth. Traction's record of purchasing new vehicles was better than Glenvale's, but its fleet was still relatively old overall and was most definitely very mixed. A few Stagecoach cast-offs —

Left: One of the victims of the deal between Stagecoach and Citylink was the Motorvator service which Stagecoach had used to compete with Citylink on the busy Glasgow–Edinburgh corridor. This 2004 view, featuring a Volvo B10M/Van Hool operated by Crawford of Neilston, was recorded shortly before Stagecoach took over and introduced MAN double-decker coaches. *Stewart J. Brown*

Right: A RoadCar Volvo Citybus with Alexander body leaves Lincoln bus station in the summer of 2005. The business is now owned by Stagecoach. This bus started life with Burnley & Pendle Transport. *Stewart J. Brown*

Above: A prominent Strathtay name is carried on the vehicles which Stagecoach acquired when it purchased Traction Group. This is a Dennis Dart with Northern Counties body soon after the takeover and before it had acquired a Stagecoach national fleet number. *Daniel Stazicker*

early Austrian-built Volvo B6Rs and mid-1980s Loyland Tigers (albeit rebodied) — came back to the group for, presumably, a few short months.

Within weeks buses were being repainted. The Yorkshire operations were rebranded as Stagecoach Yorkshire, while Road Car became Stagecoach Lincolnshire, but Strathtay (initially, at least) retained its fleetname. Having made big strides in updating the Merseyside fleet, the group now transferred several ex-Glenvale single-deckers to begin the process in Yorkshire.

Traction's founder, Frank Carter, wanted to retire, and Stagecoach's Brian Souter had long let it be known that he would like to acquire the business — just as he had been interested in buying the Gillmoss operation before Glenvale was set up. Traction takes Stagecoach into South Yorkshire in a big way and West Yorkshire on a smaller scale, just as the PTEs are flexing their muscles and expressing dissatisfaction with the services provided by First.

The hunger for growth didn't end with the year. By February 2006 Stagecoach Wales had acquired 29-vehicle Glyn Williams — its principal competitor in

the Eastern Valleys — in a deal that brought the first Turkish-built BMC Falcons into the group.

Within a week of the Glyn Williams purchase being announced Stagecoach had concluded another acquisition across the English border, in Gloucestershire. This comprised the bus operations of Dukes Travel, based at Coleford in the Forest of Dean, and brought to the Stagecoach West fleet 26 assorted single-deckers — one of them an MCV-bodied MAN that had been among the few new vehicles supplied to 2 Travel Group. In a situation similar to Dennis's of Dukinfield, Duke was the forename of the company's founder in the 1970s.

West Yorkshire provided First with its sole takeover of the year — the services of Black Prince Buses of Morley. Like Traction's Frank Carter, Black Prince founder Brian Crowther wanted to retire. His was probably the fleet mourned most by enthusiasts during 2005, for over the previous 20 years it had seen frequent changes, contained much variety and employed three distinct liveries. The principal colours latterly were maroon, red, black and yellow, but there were also blue buses (in homage to Samuel Ledgard, whose blue buses had served the area until 1967) and a few in two-tone-green Leeds City Transport colours. Some single-deckers — several bodied locally by Optare — had been acquired new or nearly new, but two generations of second-hand double-deckers dominated the fleet over its last dozen years. Volvo Ailsas from several sources included such one-offs as

If we didn't sense that Tellings Golden Miller's expansion plans had halted at the beginning of 2005, there was no doubt by June. Four months earlier TGM had reacquired the 36-vehicle AirLinks airside coach business at Heathrow from National Express Group, but the boot was very much on the other foot in June when it sold its London and Surrey local bus operations to NatEx's Travel London subsidiary for £20.4 million.

Travel London had grown into a 240-vehicle business by winning TfL contracts and taking over French-owned Connex Bus. The TGM deal added another 182 buses, 16 TfL contracts and 15 for Surrey County Council. While TGM had given up its ambition to become a major London bus operator, it remained a regional coach and bus operator, and its Burton's Coaches subsidiary took advantage of the collapse of Supreme Coaches in Essex to acquire the latter's Colchester depot and private-hire business.

Travel London had acquired Connex Bus from Veolia in February 2004, apparently ending the French group's unhappy involvement in the British bus and rail markets. However, while we may have seen the last of the Connex name here, the company bought its way back into the UK in the autumn, when, as Veolia Transport, it bought Bebb Travel of Llantwit Fardre. This well-respected and hitherto family-owned business had been around for 80 years and had 39 coaches and buses — the coaches on National Express contracts, the Optare Solo buses on tendered services. Veolia

hinted that this might be the first of other similar deals.

Any doubts that the French groups had long-term designs on the UK market were dispelled by the first major deal of 2006. Transdev, whose determination to acquire Yellow Buses surprised many, caused a quite different surprise by acquiring 100% of the shares in Blazefield — by now the country's largest privately owned bus group.

Blazefield had emerged from AJS Holdings, one of the first generation of bus groups to take advantage of NBC privatisation. 'AJS' were the initials of Alan Stephenson, who as Managing Director of East Yorkshire had followed the acquisition of his own company with the purchase of two of NBC's biggest basket-cases — West Yorkshire Road Car and London Country (North East).

Besides selling his stake in East Yorkshire, Alan Stephenson broke up and ultimately sold off the other companies. Two of his managers, Giles Fearnley and Stuart Wilde, formed Blazefield in 1991 to take over what was left — principally Harrogate & District, Keighley & District and Yorkshire Coastliner in the north and Sovereign in Hertfordshire and London.

Above: Although the bus is in Tellings Golden Miller's London-service livery, the Travel London fleetnames on this Mini Pointer Dart are indicative of the new order which came in during 2005. Travel London's livery is unrelieved red, as visible on the **Dart behind.** *Stewart J. Brown*

Below: Blazefield operated through a number of subsidiaries and had an innovative approach to marketing. 'The Zone' was a new image for an improved service network in Keighley, launched in 2004 with new TransBus Mini Pointer Darts. *Stewart J. Brown*

They would subsequently sell most of Sovereign to Arriva and Transdev but in 2001 expanded by setting up Lancashire United and Burnley & Pendle to take over Stagecoach's under-performing East Lancashire operations.

Besides the 'small company' strategy Blazefield also pursued another successful AJS policy of investing in new buses, which it replaced at regular intervals. Latterly, Traction Group bought many of its oldest vehicles — including far-from-old low-floor single-deckers — while others joined FirstGroup. Not only was its fleet among the newest in the country; it also was among the most adventurously specified, with leather-seated double- and single-deckers bought to tempt car drivers onto its most promising routes.

Transdev has persuaded Blazefield's owners — still in their early 50s — to stay on for at least two years and says it wants to harness their experience of commercial bus operation. This is not only for expansion in the UK but also to help Transdev apply British thinking to mainland European and other world markets.

A dozen years ago the bus industry was jolted into realising how fast things were changing when Stagecoach bought Western Travel, which until then had shown every sign of being another regional bus group set on an acquisition path of its own. Suddenly

we realised what consolidation meant. The Transdev/Blazefield deal has done the same, and shows that — just as Arriva and National Express are expanding in Europe — European groups could acquire ever larger slices of the UK bus industry. Inevitably the rumour-mill went into a high-speed spin in the immediate aftermath of the sale, with tales of Trent Barton and East Yorkshire sales gaining apparent credence simply by their repetition. Just as inevitably, those businesses will be sold sooner or later, but only history will tell us to whom.

If the events of 2005/6 tell us nothing else, it should be that nothing can be ruled out. Indeed, it would be foolish to imagine that all of the big groups will remain intact forever. They are not immune to takeovers or possibly break-ups, with maybe some regional operations being sold or even being split into separate bus and train businesses.

The process of change that began with privatisation in 1986 is by no means over, but 2005 was certainly one of its landmark years.

Above: Black double-deckers with leather seats were introduced by Harrogate & District on its limited-stop service between Ripon and Leeds, and then by Burnley & Pendle for its operation between Nelson and Manchester. These eye-catching vehicles were Volvo B7TLs with Wright Eclipse Gemini bodywork. *Stewart J. Brown*

Below: On a wintry day in December 2005 one of the oldest vehicles in the Blazefield fleets, an Alexander-bodied Volvo B10B of Harrogate & District, heads for Boroughbridge. The group would be bought by Transdev the following month. *Gary Steel*

In Search of Missing Gems

MIKE GREENWOOD describes his search for photographs of rare vehicles with Leicestershire or other personal connections.

Most enthusiasts have their favourite fleets, and many endeavour to track down photographs of every member of that fleet. Commercial suppliers and stalls at rallies have helped to make that task easier, but inevitably most enthusiasts end up with a 'hit list' of requirements.

The missing gems can materialise from all sorts of unlikely sources and may have lain undiscovered for some considerable time. The one rule for everybody who continues the search is never to give up! Here I look at just four missing gems that have been discovered in recent years and unravel the stories behind their detection.

My own specific interests are Leicester City Transport and its precedents, Midland Red (especially its Leicestershire operations) and Leicestershire independents. Photographs of Leicester's trams and buses are reasonably well covered, but one vehicle that was proving particularly difficult to track down was Leyland TD7 No 347 in single-deck form.

Leicester had received just two vehicles during the war. Both had Leyland TD7 chassis, 346 being bodied by Brush and delivered in January 1942, whilst 347 was bodied by Pickering and delivered in May 1942. During the war most bodybuilders had to make do with poor quality materials, and this must have been the case with the Pickering-bodied example, because in October 1950 Leicester took the decision to remove the top deck and staircase and create a 26-seat single-decker.

Although 347 was photographed on a number of occasions as a double-decker, it seemed that for whatever reason there was no photograph of it as a single-decker. Now remember the maxim of never giving up. My good friend Mike Jordan, BaMMOT's Midland Red photograph archivist, is constantly searching for new material for the BaMMOT archive. Occasionally amongst the Midland Red material that

Below: In its original form as a double-decker, Leicester City Transport Pickering-bodied Leyland TD7 No 347 stands outside Blackbird Road speedway stadium in July 1948. *Roy Marshall*

comes his way are photographs of vehicles of other operators.

Knowing my interest in Leicester Mike kindly redirects any relevant material in my direction. So it was that in 2004 a small package arrived in the post. In it were three photographs of Leicester buses. The first two were of O664-type AEC Renowns, which were pleasant enough but of no particular significance. However, the third picture was a real jaw-dropper! Leicester had withdrawn 347 in March 1955 and somewhat surprisingly had found a buyer in local housebuilder Jelson, which used it for staff transport. The third photograph that Mike had sent was of 347 in use with Jelson and had been taken in July 1958 — just a couple of months before the builder sold it to dealer Errington. When a photograph on the hit-list is discovered one is hopeful that it is of reasonable quality. In the case of the Jelson picture the quality was first-class.

Missing gem number two is a little bit more up to date. Bus photography became a preoccupation of the masses probably from the mid-'Sixties as 35mm photography became increasingly more affordable; photographs taken in the early 'Sixties were by no means as plentiful, and thus tracking down material still not easy. In 1997 my approach to Ian Allan Publishing to produce *Glory Days: Midland Red* was accepted, and the task to discover new previously unpublished material was well and truly on. Many enthusiasts will be aware that Midland Red built two D10 underfloor-engined double-deck prototypes, 4943

and 4944, which entered service in 1961. Initially allocated to Birmingham garages, the pair spent the final part of their lives working from Stafford garage, but in 1963/4 they spent a short period in Leicester, presumably for evaluation purposes (although by this time it had been decided not to develop the class for full production). During my quest I was fortunate in being able to examine Mike Sutcliffe's wonderful collection, and amongst the large selection of very fine material was a super shot of No 4943 in Leicester — in glorious colour, no less! The photograph was taken in March 1964 at that magnet for enthusiasts, St Margaret's bus station.

Example three is an illustration of a different strategy, when a missing gem — or in this case several missing gems — can be obtained from someone who isn't even a bus enthusiast. In 1997 I formed the Leicester Transport Study Group, whose mission in life is to research and document all facets of transport history relating to the city and county. A quarterly journal is produced, a copy of which is lodged with the Leicester, Leicestershire & Rutland Record Office, with which a good relationship has been developed. As part of the Group recruitment process a poster was displayed at the Record Office, and this was spotted by noted local family historian Tom Shaw.

Tom's grandfather was also called Thomas and happened to be the co-founder of Leicester bus

operator Kemp & Shaw. Tom's father and uncle (both also called Thomas!) had worked for the company, which was taken over by Midland Red in 1955 but operated as a subsidiary until 1959, when it was fully absorbed. Tom approached the LTSG in the hope that he might be able to discover more details about his family's activities. The cross-fertilisation was very beneficial to all parties, Tom producing seven very early photographs of Kemp & Shaw vehicles, which got local enthusiasts very excited, along with all sorts of fascinating documents and artefacts. One of the photographs is reproduced in this feature. The contact between Tom Shaw and the Group became the catalyst for the production of the Group's first publication detailing the fascinating history of Kemp & Shaw, to coincide with the 50th anniversary of the Midland Red takeover.

The final gem relates to my adopted city, Sheffield, to which I moved as part of a job change in 1983. Sheffield Transport was another proud municipal operator that has many devotees. The transport department, uniquely with its A, D and C fleets, operated countless buses and trams over the years, and not surprisingly a number have made it on to my hit-list.

One noted Sheffield (and Rotherham) historian and photo-collector is Paul Fox, who also happens to be a master of tracking down hidden gems. Paul also has an infectious sense of humour, and his account of the moment when he revealed a very significant missing gem to another collector is worth recounting.

Sheffield transport historians had long debated over the intake of 1934 Park Royal-bodied AEC Regents 261-5. Photographs of some of the batch were difficult

Above: Midland Red D10 No 4943 during its brief stay in Leicester, photographed at the city's St Margaret's bus station in March 1964. *Mike Sutcliffe collection*

Right: One of the seven gems emanating from Tom Shaw. Kemp & Shaw Daimler Y NR 163 was acquired from the Coalville Bus & Garage Co in May 1925; here Tom's father, Thomas Arthur Shaw, poses against the vehicle later the same year. It took almost 80 years for this photograph to surface and become available to photo collectors and transport historians. *Tom Shaw collection*

to locate; Nos 262-5 were part of the same build programme, so there were no particular mysteries that remained unresolved, but with 261 it was an entirely different matter. New as an AEC demonstrator, registered BMG 969, this vehicle ended its days as a single-deck AEC Regal coach, but it was impossible to find a photograph of it in original form — impossible, that is, until January 2001, when Paul Fox, inspecting some of Geoff Lumb's albums, came across a stunning photograph …

Paul is one of those good sorts who is always willing to share his triumphs with others whenever he can. One of the many beneficiaries of his endeavours is Howard Turner, another renowned Sheffield historian. Howard regularly visits Paul, and it was on his visit in early February 2001 that Paul was able to inform Howard of his latest discovery. Paul recalls the moment. 'I produced the print of BMG 969 without any of the usual build-up, passing the picture over face-up, asking simply: "Have you seen this one before?", after which there was a stunned silence, before our man shrieked and collapsed into the settee, followed by a further silence, before he gasped: "Ring for the doctor!" Recovering a little, Howard went on: "Oh! I don't believe it, Paul. I'm dreaming! I'm hallucinating!" '

You may just glean from the above that the discovery, which had taken 56 years to achieve, caused quite a stir. It also demonstrates that unearthing such gems may have serious health implications!

Now … is there anyone out there who may have a shot of Leicester City Transport Leyland PD2 No 123 or AEC Regent III No 19? Or how about a photograph of Midland Red D5B No 3824 with the Royal Shakespeare Company? The search goes on!

Left: The photograph that got Howard Turner so excited. Sheffield Transport Park Royal-bodied AEC Regent 261 (BMG 969) in Haymarket, Sheffield, on 6 November 1934. *British Commercial Vehicle Museum*

Right: BMG 969 eventually became a Regal coach, in which form it was operated by London operator Eastern Belle, of Bow. *Howard Turner collection*

Advancing in a Forward Direction

Do we always learn lessons from the past? GAVIN BOOTH looks back.

Nostalgia, famously, is not what it was. In the same way that retired colonels in Surrey used to complain that the long-running humorous weekly *Punch* was 'not as funny as it used to be' (to which the popular riposte was: 'it never was'), I pose the question: were older buses really as good as we sometimes think?

Now there are those who might think that, as founding editor of *Classic Bus* magazine, I would have no time for modern buses, that I would espouse the case for a return to good old-fashioned values, and that I would have been found lying across the entrance to Brixton garage on 9 December 2005 to prevent the last normal-service Routemaster on the 159 from completing its final journey. Sorry to disappoint, but the answer in every case is 'no'.

I accept the premise that it is great to be nostalgic about the past — indeed, I've made my living for the past 13 years doing just that — but we have to move on. As one of my old bosses at the Scottish Bus Group, Roddy MacKenzie, said in an interview for *Commercial Motor* magazine about SBG's vehicle-buying policy, 'We must advance, but only in a forward direction'.

So, instead of simply getting misty-eyed about halfcabs and conductors, it is possible to look at a modern bus and recognise just how much the vehicles and the industry have advanced. And in a forward direction too.

Looking at the UK bus industry's history, it is possible to identify many situations where today's industry — operators and manufacturers alike — has benefited from the things that happened over the first century of motor-bus operation in the UK. Sometimes it is clear that the industry has recognised good practices from the past and has built on these; on other occasions it has looked back and resolved never to make the same mistakes again.

Take the Routemaster, which is a good example. I made my last normal trip on a London Routemaster a few days before the brouhaha that surrounded The Last Day — well, Last Days, actually.

It was busy, noisy, cramped. The cover strapline for

All photographs by the author

Classic Bus magazine came to mind: 'Remembering Buses The Way They Used To Be'. That summed it up. I wanted to remember Routemasters in the world for which they were designed — back in the 1960s, when they seemed to be ideal for London conditions — not as clapped-out, scruffy buses that had passed their sell-by dates.

As editor of *Classic Bus* I was expected by some readers to have no time for modern vehicles, to mourn the passing of buses like the Routemaster and to criticise modern 'soulless boxes'. But that's not for me. I get just as excited by Lothian's latest Volvo/Geminis as I did 50 years ago by Edinburgh's PD2/Orions.

Back to my Routemaster. This is a good example of learning from the past. It was conceived as a trolleybus replacement, was a long time in development, as was London Transport's way, and by the time it had entered service in quantity a new generation of buses had caught up — buses that were longer, with more seats and with their engines at the back.

By any standards the RM was a remarkable bus, but it may have outlasted its welcome. What did the industry learn from the RM? Apart from the need for a shorter development phase, under its traditional exterior was a range of technical innovations; the RM gave the rest of the industry first-hand experience of intensive use of such novel features as automatic gearboxes, power steering, air suspension and aluminium construction.

But the world into which the Routemaster was born was very different from the world that witnessed its very public funeral. Buses rarely make the national news unless they crash or are blown up, so the attention given to the Routemaster's demise was perhaps a little surprising, and nonetheless touching, even if some of the media coverage seemed determined to place it in a London that no longer exists, a London of Pearly Kings and Queens, New Elizabethan hope, chirpy cabbies and costermongers' barrows.

Now I'm not anti-Routemaster. Far from it; nearly 50

years ago I dragged my long-suffering parents and sister to Surrey Docks in an ultimately successful bid to find and ride on RM1. I sought out Routemasters in those early trolleybus-replacement days and have ridden on them on countless occasions in London and in many other surprising parts of the UK; I've driven them too — on one occasion a Mac Tours example all the way from Edinburgh to London to take part in the RM50 event at Finsbury Park in 2004. But that doesn't mean that they're 21st-century buses, other than for heritage work, or even 1990s or (whisper it) 1980s buses either.

Back in 1959, when RMs first entered squadron service, we accepted what we had because we didn't know any better, but I wouldn't welcome a Tardis ride back to the world of 1959, back to a world when phones were black bakelite things, when television was black-and-white and the channel choice was BBC or ITV, when the Austin Cambridge was regarded as a sensible family car, when computers were so large they needed special buildings, and when we had never heard of The Beatles.

If I want to relive these days I can listen to pop music from the time on a CD covering that era. Not, of course, CDs bought at the time; they didn't exist. I could listen to the same music on vinyl bought at the time, but CDs are so much easier to use, and the sound quality is so much better.

And I would use the same argument about Routemasters: would I prefer to be sitting upstairs (among people who, like myself, are rather bigger and probably broader of beam than in the 1950s), in a Routemaster or in a nice new Volvo/Gemini or a Mercedes-Benz artic? As a passenger I'd prefer the newer buses, even the much-derided 'Hendy's Bendys', which I was amused to see referred to, in the context of Routemaster withdrawal, as 'Satan's Squeezeboxes'.

If they are sensible, busmen take note of the successes and failures of the past.

Read some of the books that detail the history of bus operators and you realise that there is much to be learned from the past; you occasionally feel these should be required reading for some of today's entrepreneurial busmen. You recognise the risks that were taken in the early days of the motor-bus industry and how some paid off and others led to slow decline. Passenger-transport history has a habit of repeating previous successes and failures. You can see clear parallels between the phenomenal period of growth in the 1920s and 1930s and the revitalised bus industry of the past 20 years.

The roots of my old employer, the Scottish Bus Group, were planted in the 1920s and 1930s. A lot of people saw a future for bus travel, and remember that in the 1920s entry to the industry was cheap and easy. Most operators foundered along the way, selling out to — or giving up in the face of — competition from the handful of companies that rose to the top of the pile.

In Scotland three families dominated the scene — the Alexanders in central Scotland, the Dicks in Lanarkshire and the Swords in the west of Scotland. Stagecoach's Brian Souter would have felt very much at home in any of these companies and in the

Right: The Routemaster as many will prefer to remember the type: a smartly presented RM1563 at Charing Cross in 1982, by which time, based on the original thinking, it would have been in its last days of London service.

buses have been a popular tool for competitive services because in theory they were cheaper to buy and cheaper to run. Indeed, the cut-throat bus wars of the 1920s that led to regulation in 1930 were often waged with small buses, typically imports from Europe and the United States.

The advent of greater controls, including route licensing, from 1930 put paid to the out-and-out competition, and this suppressed the market for smaller buses. In the new regulated world most operators were investing in larger buses to meet the steadily growing demand for public transport. But there was still a limited demand for smaller buses, which prewar was met by buses like Bedfords, and models like the Dennis Ace and Dart, and the Leyland Cub.

Above: The Seddon Pennine IV-236, better remembered as the Midi, was an early attempt to provide a scaled-down large bus for urban duties. In the 1970s Greater Manchester PTE used Midis on the Centreline service linking Manchester's Piccadilly and Victoria railway stations with the city centre.

In the healthy market for bus travel after the war manufacturers not surprisingly concentrated on big buses, and operators looking for something smaller often turned to chassis like the Bedford OB. But as costs rose and passenger numbers started to decline in the 1950s, some larger operators started looking for small buses, usually so they could use them on a driver-only basis. Different manufacturers came up with different solutions — Dennis produced the normal-control Falcon for Aldershot & District and East Kent, Guy produced the normal-control GS-type for London Transport, Albion adapted its underfloor-engined Claymore goods chassis to produce the Nimbus, and Bristol developed the front-engined SC and later the underfloor-engined SU.

In the 1960s Bedford introduced the VAS for small buses and coaches, but in the 1970s Seddon, which had enjoyed but limited success on the home market with its bus and coach models, produced a complete new small bus, officially the 6.5m-long Pennine IV-236, but cleverly dubbed the Midi, introducing a class description that is still in use today. The Midi had a front engine, with a front entrance ahead of the front axle, and the standard body, built by Seddon's in-house bodybuilder, Pennine Coachcraft, gave it a neat, purpose-built appearance.

Bristol offered the LHS, a shortened LH, and this was bought by NBC fleets and by London Transport. A small bus that might have been a winner had it appeared a few years later was the Bedford JJL, an extremely stylish 27-seat rear-engined bus developed by Bedford from Marshall ideas. The UK market wasn't ready for the JJL when it appeared in 1978, but a decade or so later it could well have given the Dart a hard time. But by then General Motors, Bedford's parent, wasn't greatly interested in the UK bus market.

Deregulation opened the floodgates, with fleets of all sizes buying Transits and Sherpas, and later various Dodge and Mercedes-Benz models, to provide high-frequency customer-friendly services. Buses of this size were unfamiliar to many fleets and to many engineers, who resolved to get rid of them as quickly as they could.

Many fleets learned the hard way from their experiences of van-derived minibuses, the oft-criticised 'breadvans', that smaller buses had a place but had to be up to the punishing work schedule expected of them. And it took a while for some manufacturers to accept that something designed as a van needed to be beefed up before it could be used successfully as a bus. Even the worst excesses of White Van Man are no match for the stop-start world of local buses and the strain this puts on engine, gearbox and brakes.

This prompted the second phase of minibuses, which introduced the MCW Metrorider, a sturdier

Left: Harry Blundred famously introduced high-frequency minibuses in Exeter, which is acknowledged as the cradle of the 1980s minibus revolution. This Ford Transit in the Devon General fleet is seen in Exeter High Street in one of several route-specific liveries.

purpose-built bus, and the Dennis Domino, a scaled-down Dominator and consequently a substantial piece of kit. The Metrorider survived the end of MCW bus production to re-emerge as the Optare MetroRider. The Domino was closer to the perhaps misguided European concept of a small bus — a scaled-down big bus — and must have helped convince Dennis that what people wanted was a small bus designed from the ground up, with reliable components and a feeling of size and space. That, of course, would emerge in 1988 as the Dart. As one of the best-selling British bus chassis of all time, the Dart learned a lot from the earlier attempts to crack this market.

That entry to the bus industry is so easy is both good and bad. It's good that the industry has moved away from the inefficiencies of regulation and state

ownership. Scottish Bus Group was great on the supply side. The engineers specified the buses, so they were solid, reliable and easy to work on; forget that they were often difficult to use and had all the internal appeal of a hospital corridor. But the engineers were good at keeping them on the road and the traffic people were good at scheduling and staffing them. Never mind that they sometimes ran at times to suit the bus company and didn't necessarily go to the places that people wanted.

This ease of entry means that while there are pockets of slightly dubious operation — places like Greenock and Paisley spring to mind — there are many more cases where the freedoms of deregulation have led to greatly improved bus services and have encouraged exciting innovation. From my local bus

Left: Minibuses were soon to be seen in many traditional 'big bus' fleets, like Brighton & Hove, one of whose Mercedes-Benz L608Ds is seen high above Brighton in 1986.

Below: A later generation of Greater Manchester Centreline buses was the batch of 20 Dennis Dominos with Northern Counties bodywork bought in 1985/6. They were rather like scaled-down Dominators but perhaps paved the way for the Dennis Dart just a few years later.

Above: Many operators progressed from minibuses to the Dennis Dart, which became Britain's best-selling chassis. Many had Plaxton Pointer bodies; this shorter-length MPD version is one of a large fleet of Darts built up by Cardiff Bus.

Below: Deregulation allowed anybody with suitable qualifications to start up a bus service, possibly in competition with a larger operator. Lothian Transit did this in Edinburgh, using this former SBG Leyland Leopard/Alexander Y type on Lothian's route 10, though Lothian responded with Leyland Lynxes that shadowed the Leopard; one can be seen on the right.

Left: Edinburgh's 1.5km-long guided busway is served by Lothian Buses Volvo B7RLE/Wright single-deckers and Dennis Trident/Plaxton double-deckers. A B7RLE picks up passengers at one of the 'stations' on the busway.

stop I enjoy 40 buses an hour into Edinburgh city centre — yes, 40 — including one service on a five-minute frequency. One of the successes of my local operator, Lothian Buses, is route 22, which as this is written is due to increase from a five-minute to a four-minute frequency, and even on Sundays it runs every 10 minutes from 10 in the morning until 11 at night.

Lothian is one operator prepared to learn from the past, helped by senior managers who are more than a little interested in buses. One of Neil Renilson's first actions when he took over as Chief Executive in 1999 was to start a revamp of the city's bus network. As an Edinburgh native he knew that it had been getting more and more complicated, with variations and sub-variations to confuse even the regular passengers. So he dug out a map of the Edinburgh tramway system — just 28 routes covering a city that has grown considerably at the fringes since the trams went nearly

50 years ago. He recognised that people still recalled the route numbers of the trams, and although today's routes travel considerably beyond the tram termini of old, for the main city sections he tweaked routes to take account of the changing city, but ensured that familiar route numbers were used. When new bus services are introduced, Lothian is careful to use numbers that have some historical significance. Lothian acknowledges that the people who planned the tramway network more than a century ago knew what they were doing.

Looking back, learning from the past, it is possible to recognise that there was a need to move on from what had been convenient and comfortable. The changes of the 1980s have created a bus industry that, while certainly not perfect, is probably healthier than it has been for many years.

Advancing in a forward direction, in fact.

Left: The UK's other major guided busway is in East Leeds, where three Volvo B7TL/Alexander ALX400s, two from the First fleet and the other Arriva, are seen heading out of Leeds city centre in 2002.

Right: Unguided busway, the Dutch way. A Van Hool AG300 artic on the 25km Zuidtangent busway approaches the interchange at Hoofdorp railway station, with an NS double-deck inter-city train in the background.

Left: The Dutch Zuidtangent busway provides the facilities of a tramway without the high capital costs but could be upgraded to light rail in the future. The station platforms are at Hoofdorp, where Zuidtangent connects with the Dutch railway network.

Right: Simpler than Zuidtangent, the unguided busway in suburban Utrecht, served by the double-articulated 25m-long Van Hool AGG300s from the Utrecht municipal fleet.

Above: Larger groups have the resources to experiment with new concepts. Grampian, predecessor of First, bought this Mercedes-Benz O405G with Alexander body, to test articulated buses. It is seen in Aberdeen in 1993.

Below: First went on to embrace articulated buses in a fairly big way, and has developed its 'ftr' concept vehicle, designed to be used on suitable 'track', in conjunction with local authorities. The vehicle is an adapted Volvo B7LA, with the front axle set forward, and carries bodywork by Wrightbus, which calls it the StreetCar. The first StreetCar is seen on demonstration in Edinburgh in 2005.

Park & Ride

Park-and-ride services are a popular means of tackling congestion in towns and cities around Britain. TONY WILSON illustrates a variety of operations — and reveals that the concept is not a new one.

Variety

All photographs by the author

Park-and-ride schemes abound nowadays. Most of our major towns and cities either already have or are considering introducing this type of operation to ease the increasing problem of traffic congestion. The majority of these facilities are operated all year round. However, additionally there are others created for specific events and run for limited periods. These may be for events such as annual county shows, exhibitions, seasonal events and sports meetings, among other things.

Take Norwich, for example, where a network of park-and-ride services has been developed to move passengers from several sites situated at strategic locations on the outskirts to the city centre.

The operation here, as in many other cities, uses vehicles of a very high standard. Each route and car park is defined by a colour code that extends to the buses, leaving the passenger in no doubt as to which vehicle to catch to return to the parking area from the city centre.

The fare system in Norwich indicates the attractive offers made to encourage drivers to use park-and-ride services. In 2005 for £2.80 (or £1.00 Monday to Friday after 12.30pm) up to five adults and three children could travel on production of their car-park ticket. Furthermore, disabled drivers and their passengers could travel free on production of their Blue Badge, the time card being used to identify the owner's vehicle

Right: Down in the West Country a Western National Bristol SUL with ECW body trundles back into Falmouth from the park-and-ride site on the edge of the town in July 1978, demonstrating that there's nothing new in the concept. The vehicle sports a rather apt COD registration, considering the town's location on Cornwall's south coast, where a large fishing fleet was based at the time.

in the secure parking area. All six sites are secure, with CCTV cover and pleasant, purpose-built waiting facilities. Not that waiting is long. Indeed, buses operate at such frequencies that it is rare to find the bus stand without a vehicle waiting. This sort of operation — which is not unique to Norwich — must be the way forward to tempt drivers out of their cars. Coincidentally, Norwich is now the proud possessor of a brand-new bus station, to which all the routes operate.

Whilst the East Anglian city may be among the latest of a number of park-and-ride operations to spring up in recent years, it is surprising just how long such services have been around. It was way back in 1978 that a little Bristol single-decker attracted this photographer's eye operating such a service in the Cornish town of Falmouth. Some time later a larger coach in South Wales passed before the same lens, again back in the good old days of the National Bus Company. Since then there have been all sorts of networks introduced into many towns and cities around Britain. These range in size from the group of six routes for Norwich to a converted milk-float operation in Polperro. Vehicles on mainstream park-and-ride operations are typically new low-floor single-deckers, although on some busy services — as in Oxford, Norwich and Cambridge — double-deckers have been used.

Left: Still in the West Country but over the border in Devon a Western National Bristol FLF arrives at the riverside terminus of the Dartmouth park-and-ride service in August 1981. Whilst the destination display is unused, apart from 'Western National' appearing in the top part, advertising on the sides clearly signifies what the bus is doing.

Right: Two companies provide vehicles on several routes for Exeter's park-and-ride network. The smallest buses used are on the PR4 to and from Sowton, on the east side of the city, and these are operated by Cooks Coaches of Wellington, which lies over the border in Somerset. This is one of its fleet of long-wheelbase Optare Solos. On the other services Stagecoach Devon provides larger vehicles in the shape of Dennis Darts and Dennis Trident double-deckers.

Above: The opening of a major tourist attraction near St Austell in Cornwall required the introduction of an internal park-and-ride service. From day one the Eden Project drew huge crowds that needed to be moved from the car parking area to the main entrance. The contract was awarded to Truronian, which commenced operation with older vehicles until more modern single-deck types appeared in the shape of TransBus Enviro300s. Before their arrival one of the vehicles used was this aged Bristol VRT which had been new to Maidstone & District. It is seen in 2002.

Below: The main car park in Polperro is at the top end of the main street leading down to the harbour. In order to keep this narrow thoroughfare free from unnecessary traffic the local council kept access to a minimum. To provide transport for those who required it, two alternative forms of conveyance were in use during the 1997 summer season. Both were environmentally friendly, one being a horse-drawn carriage, the other a converted electric milk-float.

Above: During 2004 the favoured vehicle for Salisbury's park-and-ride services was the Optare Excel, operated by Wilts & Dorset. One heads for the north side of the city and the parking location known as the Beehive site. More recently Wilts & Dorset has bought Wright-bodied Volvos for park-and-ride services.

Below: A 1968 Plaxton Panorama-bodied Leyland Leopard operated by NBC's South Wales subsidiary, seen on the outskirts of Swansea. The coach is awaiting custom on the long cross-city service that linked Brynmill, on the coast, with Landore, to the northeast. The coach was new to Trent.

Above: Chronic traffic congestion in Oxford was something that desperately needed to be addressed. The layout of the city streets could not cope with the buses, let alone the car traffic. It has been more than 30 years since the introduction of the city's first park-and-ride service; this June 1980 view features an ex-London Transport Daimler Fleetline operated by NBC's City of Oxford subsidiary. It is seen on the approach road to the Peartree site, situated on the north side of the city near the junction of the A34 and the A40 trunk roads and still in use today.

Below: Oxford's park-and-ride services are still operated by City of Oxford, now trading as the Oxford Bus Company and part of Go-Ahead Group. The company took delivery of some the first Dennis Tridents to operate outside London, receiving a batch of 20 with dual-door Alexander ALX400 bodywork in the summer of 1999. One is seen heading along St Giles towards the city centre in August of that year.

Left: In more recent years, as the number of park-and-ride sites in Oxford increased and a network of bus routes was introduced to service them, so the specification of the vehicles was improved. Here an Oxford Bus Company Mercedes-Benz Citaro awaits departure from the Thornhill site on the main A40 trunk road on the London side of the city.

Right: Thames Transit has also operated park-and-ride — or 'Park & Glide' — services in Oxford, as demonstrated by this Mellor-bodied Iveco in the city centre in 1996.

Left: In that other major bastion of academia, Cambridge, park-and-ride services are operated by Stagecoach, using a fleet of differently liveried Dennis Tridents cascaded from London. Prior to this the operation was covered by a fleet of step-entrance Dennis Darts with Alexander Dash bodywork. This 1996 view was recorded in the city centre.

Above: Norfolk County Council currently runs two of the routes in the Norwich park-and-ride network, using a fleet of 14 Irisbus Agora Line single-deckers — the only significant concentration of this type in Britain. Some are in red livery for the Postwick service, others in this bright yellow for the route to Norwich Airport.

Below: Another two routes are run by Konectbus, a relatively new company in terms of mainstream bus operation. That to/from Thickthorn is operated with pink-liveried VDL DB250/Wright Pulsar Gemini double-deckers, the Costessey route using green Optare Tempos. Here one of the latter prepares to depart from Norwich's magnificent new bus station, with a pink VDL on the stand behind.

Above: The National Exhibition Centre, in the West Midlands, occupies a vast area near the M6 and M42 motorways. With an event in progress on most days of the year and being located conveniently in the middle of England, it attracts many visitors in cars. To cater for them, huge vehicle parks were created, served by a network of park-and-ride routes. During the late 1990s the contract for these services was held by Flights Travel Group, which used a fleet of low-floor Dennis Darts with Plaxton Pointer bodywork and FTG registrations.

Below: Nottingham has long had park-and-ride services, Nottingham City Transport, Trent Barton and Dunn-Line all providing buses over the years. Here one of Dunn-Line's small fleet of East Lancs-bodied Dennis Darts passes through the city centre before heading out to the Racecourse site on the south side of the city in April 1997. Nottingham's park-and-ride services have been altered significantly following the introduction of the city's new tram system.

Right: One of the more unusual short-term park-and-ride schemes can be found in Derbyshire. The annual two-day Bakewell Show in early August attracts thousands of visitors from miles around, many of whom arrive by car. For many years disused railway lines have been used as bridleways and footpaths, and one of these is put to good use during this period. Suspended for the duration, the Monsal Trail becomes a bus-only track enabling buses to run freely between a temporary car park at the old Hassop railway station and another in Bakewell itself. About to pass beneath the bridge carrying the main road between Bakewell and Baslow, a Bedford YNT/Duple 320 operated by Hulley's of Baslow trundles down the former trackbed in 1994.

Left: Concerned at increasing traffic levels in their town, the citizens of Kendal in Cumbria were moved to introduce a free bus service linking car parks and the shops at the height of the tourist season. Initially operated by a couple of minibuses, the service has in more recent times been run by Cumbria Classic Coaches. As the name suggests, this is not a modern fleet, and the use of a vintage vehicle certainly pulled in the customers. In particularly unseasonal weather in September 1999 one of the operator's Leyland Tigers, with Alexander bodywork, prepares to leave the parking area adjacent to the K Village shopping outlet, formerly a shoe factory.

Right: In the town of Alnwick, already a magnet for visitors, the major development of a derelict 12-acre walled garden within the castle gardens by the Duchess of Northumberland has in recent years become a huge success — so much so that something had to be done about the large number of visiting vehicles. In 2002 a park-and-ride service was introduced, the contract being awarded initially to local operator Dreadnought Coaches, which included in its small but interesting fleet this ex-London Fleetline, waiting to begin a journey from the parking site to the gardens in August 2003.

Above: Introduced in Edinburgh during 2006 was route X48 linking the city centre with a purpose-built parking area to the west. A 25-minute ride in one of Lothian Buses' low-floor Dennis Darts takes passengers along stretches of the city's 'Greenway', part of an intended network of road upgrades to speed the passage of buses.

Below: Possibly the most northerly full-time park-and-ride service is that in Aberdeen. In 1995 it was being operated by Grampian Regional Transport (now First Aberdeen) using Optare-bodied Mercedes-Benz O405s with attractive City Quick branding.

Lies, Damned Lies ... and Digital

All photographs by the author

A lot has changed in the bus world during the three years since PETER ROWLANDS started taking digital photographs — and he has learned how to change it further. Here he reflects on the opportunities and temptations of the digital era.

"This reprint you've just done for me — I appreciate your efforts, but it doesn't look anything like the original. The colours are completely different."

The man in the photographic shop casts a fleeting, unseeing glance at the six-by-four I've just slid out of its yellow sleeve, then stares back at me, unmoving.

"No they're not."

"But Grimsby buses are orange, not vermilion!"

"I don't know anything about that."

"But you had the original to compare with. Couldn't you have followed that?"

"We used the settings our machine gave us. The machine gives the ideal result." He might as well have said "Computer says no", except that they didn't consider them computers in those days.

"But can't you engage brain as well?"

To my shame, I never actually added that last comment, but there were many times when I wished I dared. It's a scenario we've all been through at one time or another: trying in vain to get the photographic shop to reproduce an image that their machine managed to create perfectly well first time around but which it seems obstinately incapable of repeating.

Traditional photography was basically a lottery. I sometimes wonder how I stuck it all those years. Even first-run prints weren't always ideal. Far too often you'd hurry home with an eagerly awaited packet of prints only to find they had a peculiar cast that wasn't evident under the shop lighting. Or the whole film was printed at a machine setting suitable for the few sunny-day shots, even though most of the pictures were taken on another, duller day and had come out far too dark.

My photographic archives are stuffed with bus pictures that I've never seen in their full glory, and quite probably never will — images that could have been printed far better if I'd had the energy to insist on a proper result, or the lab had been more conscientious. It became a game of attrition; the shops almost dared you to protest and land yourself with further trips into town, further raised blood pressure, further frustration.

Not any more! Digital has done away with all that. Suddenly we have the power again. We can brighten, darken, distort, tweak and change our pictures to our hearts' content. It's nothing less than a revolution, and in a way I find myself wondering why it took me so long to convert.

But convert I did. On 8 February 2003 I stepped out into Fulham High Street and took what now seems to me a rather momentous photograph — my first-ever digital bus picture. And I haven't taken a single conventional photograph ever since.

With the benefit of hindsight, I now know it was momentous in more ways than one. It was also the first in a countdown of photographs that I took in the last three years of mainstream Routemaster operation in London. When I took it the whole surviving fleet was still running intact on 20 routes and looked set to continue indefinitely. As I write this, in February 2006, they have all gone.

It's a sobering thought that so much can change in such a relatively short time. Now that I come to look, other pictures taken during those three years also reflect the subtle but ceaseless evolution of the industry — changes in livery, in operators, in vehicles. It's also chastening to realise just how quickly it can become almost a routine to change such scenes yourself in order to end up with a better result. Change electronically, I mean — that's the wonder of digital photography, of course. We're moving rapidly into a world where lamp-posts no longer protrude from bus roofs; where plastic bags never waft under the wheels; where grimy skirt panels are a thing of the past.

Whether this kind of visual editing is legitimate or not is another matter. You could maintain that 'Photoshopping' is distorting reality, and I wouldn't really argue. I think the end probably justifies the means, but you might take a different view.

Liberation

Probably the first thing you learn about digital photography is that it's FREE. Well, perhaps not quite;

41

Left: Since this picture was taken in April 2003 the contract to run the W8 in Enfield has been won by Metroline. More to the point, First London no longer runs this rare Dennis Arrow with Northern Counties Palatine bodywork and no longer has any front line buses in Capital Citybus yellow. Two women who were crossing the street to the left of the bus have been cloned out of the shot.

Right and below: This Alexander-bodied Volvo B7TL is seen in Maidstone, in July 2004, on one of the first days in service of Arriva's sparkling new double-decker fleet. (Not on *the* first day though.) A man drawing money from a cashpoint machine beyond it seemed a bit of a distraction, so he had to go. But as there was no model to hand for an unattended cashpoint machine this had to be replaced by cloned brickwork. A lamp-post has been removed too.

Right and below: No, this bus hasn't been cloned into a new livery. (That really would have been asking a bit much.) The operator brought that about of its own accord. Dennis's, a small company running in Manchester, was still independent when this view of a Dennis Trident with East Lancs bodywork was taken in May 2003, just off Piccadilly. By August 2005 its sister bus was in full Stagecoach livery, and the identity of its former operator was little more than a memory.

ugly and artificial. Happily, modern-day retouching should be virtually undetectable, at least to passing scrutiny.

But is this retouching acceptable in a philosophical sense? When it comes to recomposing reality, I think the jury's out. If, in truth, there was a lamp-post in view behind the bus at the precise position where you pressed the button, who's to know? Absolute reality is almost impossible to monitor. If you'd been a fraction closer to the bus, and therefore shooting at a wider angle, your foreground image (the bus) would have

filled more of the image area and might have blocked out the offending object anyway. Who can possibly check up on you?

On the other hand, if your picture ends up looking a blatant lie (lamp-posts in view through the bus windows, perhaps, but not sticking out the top), then you've let yourself down and produced a flawed work. In a way, perhaps the end justifies the means. If no-one can tell you've cleaned up your image, is there any harm?

Blinds

January 2005, and I'm on Putney Bridge, out looking for Routemasters again. By now there are only about half a dozen routes left, and this will be their last year in full service, so I'm looking for a nice defining shot.

Along comes a 14, looking remarkably smart in the bright winter sunshine, thanks (ironically) to a recent repainting programme. I get my shot, but when I look at it back on my computer I find there are several flaws. For a start, two of the destination blinds are slightly out of position. And a downstairs passenger is holding some kind of large piece of white plasterboard or something, which makes the interior look rather odd.

Oh, and while I'm about it, the driver's newspaper is stuffed in front of the steering column, cluttering up the windscreen. And the shadow on the side cast by a lamp-post is slightly obtrusive.

Most of the clutter can be sorted out by cloning. The main destination indicator is trickier; part of it has been scrolled up out of sight, and you can't easily reconstitute something that isn't there in the first place.

The answer here is to copy it from somewhere else. Fortunately in my repertoire of Routemaster pictures I find one of another 14 bound for Putney, taken the previous year in Piccadilly. So it's possible to cut out its destination-blind area, drag it to the right position in the target picture and paste it back in place. It's then relatively easy to fill in the blank bits by cloning some appropriate colour from a nearby part of the picture.

Come to think of it, what about a proper radiator

Left and below: The date — 8 January 2005 — is one of the few truthful aspects of this picture. The main destination blind was borrowed from a picture taken the previous year, and the radiator badge came from another one. The '14' is genuine but had to be scrolled down a bit. The driver's newspaper has been scrubbed out, as has a face half in view upstairs. And an unidentified white board inside the front of the saloon has been replaced by non-specific shadow.

Right: A surprisingly historic picture on many levels, this view of an Alexander-bodied Volvo Olympian was taken in Enfield Town in April 2003, when a whole plethora of other types, even midibuses, could also be seen on the route. Since a subsequent contract renewal the route has been taken over by a single type (Plaxton-bodied Trident), and Olympians have completely faded out of the London scene. Did the author wind down the final destination indicator a fraction? He's not saying.

badge to slot into the blank space on this bus? I find a suitable one on a 159 (as it happens), taken in Oxford Street in July 2003. Is it authentic though? Pass. At least it looks better than the vacant triangle shape it replaces, which was never standard for London General anyway.

Admittedly, the lighting may be subtly different in the donor fragment, but you can sometimes tone it up or down to suit and even change the colours slightly.

Incidentally, if nothing else, this technique is a rather good justification for taking a lot of otherwise similar photographs. So long as your replacement image fragment is in more or less the right perspective, you should be able to skew it into exactly the required shape in Photoshop or a similar application. But if it's completely different you'll have a struggle.

Second-guessing
Whilst no professional, I've done a bit of commissioned bus-press photography over the years, and here the

ability to retouch the image is invaluable. Even if you yourself are quite happy with prominent reflections in bus windscreens and festoons of overhead cables dangling over the vehicle, the customer might not be. You may also need to cater for the prejudices of a picture editor or page designer. It can pay to do a bit of second-guessing.

That's why commissioned jobs tend to prompt me into my most frenzied Photoshopping sessions. By the time I've cleared mud off the skirt panels, reflections off the windows and stickers from the windscreen, I feel as exercised as any cleaner.

On one occasion, in pursuit of a convenient location for photographs, I was advised by a bus driver to try some parkland near the centre of Windsor. Sure enough, I got some appropriate-looking shots and even included the castle in the background. Then I suffered a major failure of nerve. The bus was destined for a route that wouldn't take it anywhere near Windsor, and the castle was too much of a give-away. Fortunately it

Right: The Woking–Byfleet service operated by Centra with this Mercedes-Benz Citaro does not pass Windsor Castle, which was visible in the background before being faded into the mist.

was a misty day, and the walls were already indistinct. I just had to help them a little on their way to invisibility.

I confronted one of my biggest challenges when trying to photograph a midi-coach on Lambeth Bridge. The client wanted a classic picture with the Houses of Parliament in the background, but for some reason I simply couldn't get the angle right. And traffic constantly interrupted, so the driver had to keep pulling off and circumnavigating the roundabouts at both ends of the bridge in order to get back into position.

Eventually I felt as if we'd got as good as we were going to get; but when I reviewed the results later on, the best shot was marred by the prominent tower surmounting Westminster Hall. It loomed behind the coach, a great gothic obelisk soaring out of the roof. Although it was possibly my cheekiest bit of cloning yet, I was forced to the conclusion that the whole tower had to go. At a few strokes an entire building was obliterated.

Straight and narrow

It's always gratifying to take pictures of buses on their first or last day of operation. Whilst I don't necessarily go out of my way to take them, I can't help feeling pleased with myself when I do. But have you ever been tempted to pass off a picture that you took on the *second* day as if it had been taken on the first, or the second-last instead of the last? If so, watch out for EXIF!

The term is shorthand for Exchangeable Image File, a Japanese standard that defines various bits of information that your camera automatically embeds in your photographs. These include aperture, depth of field, speed setting and so on — and also the date on which the picture was taken. It appears in both TIF and JPEG files.

You can rename your file, copy it, change the compression level and do all sorts of other things with it, yet the tenacious EXIF information stays with it. Save it as a BMP, and the data appears to have vanished, but save the new image back as JPEG and lo! — the offending data is still there. Don't confuse this stuff with the ordinary system-file creation date, by the way. You can change that simply by resaving and playing around with the file; but the give-away EXIF information will still be buried deep inside.

If you want to cover your tracks, you'll find that some photo-editing software offers you the chance to amend or delete these EXIF details. If yours doesn't, look on Google for a rather neat free utility called Exifer that does the same thing. Not that I would, of course. Oh no.

Of course, EXIF data is amazingly useful if you want to check your own photographic records. How many of us have made a practice of keeping notes of the exposure we give every single picture? Nowadays we don't have to, it's recorded automatically. And the embedded date leaves you in no doubt about when you really did take the picture, whatever you might tell the rest of the world …

Clearly you couldn't pass off fraudulent pictures at high-profile events such as the last Routemaster journey on the 159. Unique event, unique bus; and the shots I got that day in Oxford Street will always occupy a proud place in my collection. I hardly even needed to retouch them — just brighten them up a bit. And I don't need the EXIF data, true or 'edited', to prove the date I took them. Some things you just can't fake.

Left: Unedited and unadorned. Seen on 9 December 2005 pulling away from the madding crowds of press photographers, enthusiasts and well-wishers in Oxford Street, RM2217 heads proudly off on its final journey into the history books. No faking this.

All Change in Colchester

The last few years have seen big changes in Colchester. GEOFF MILLS illustrates the transition from Arriva Colchester to Network Colchester.

All photographs by the author

For what was once a small municipal bus fleet, locally run like all such operations, Colchester Borough Transport has undergone remarkable changes in the last two decades. Twenty years ago it was simply CBT, at that stage an 'arm's length' company owned by the council, as required by the 1985 Transport Act. In 1993 the company was bought by British Bus and was then managed from the head office of British Bus subsidiary London & Country at Reigate, 80 miles distant.

In 1997 British Bus was acquired by the Cowie group, and control of the Colchester business returned to Essex — but not to Colchester. Instead it was managed from the Harlow offices of Cowie's County Bus subsidiary, some 35 miles away.

Cowie metamorphosed into Arriva, and in April 1998 the business was renamed Arriva Colchester, control moving from Essex to Bedfordshire, to the Luton offices of Arriva The Shires, 45 miles away.

Then came changes at Arriva, which saw the Colchester operation being managed from south of the Thames — by Arriva Southern Counties in Maidstone, 75 miles distant.

The final change came in August 2004, when Arriva gave up what was a small and geographically isolated operation, selling the Colchester business to the TGM group, which manages it from Haverhill in Suffolk, the headquarters of its Burton's Coaches business — and just 30 miles away.

Below: In its final years in municipal ownership Colchester Borough Transport bought Leyland Olympians with ECW bodies. One of three delivered in 1991 is seen in Arriva ownership in 2000. All three survived in service with Network Colchester in 2006.

Above: Only the Arriva name under the windscreen reveals that this ECW-bodied Leyland Atlantean in traditional Colchester livery isn't quite as it appears. New to Colchester Borough Transport in 1975, it was converted to open-top in 1989 and continued in use until 2000, when Arriva ceased open-top operation in the town. This photograph was taken during its last summer in service.

Below: Ownership of Colchester's buses by Arriva brought some far-travelled vehicles to the fleet. This comparatively rare Volvo B6 with Alexander Dash body had started life in Scotland in 1994 with Clydeside Buses, which business became Arriva Scotland West in 1998. The bus then headed south to Arriva The Shires and operated in Colchester from 2001 to 2005.

Top: This B6 with Northern Counties body was a one-off in the Colchester fleet. New to Kentish Bus in 1994, it reached Colchester in 2003 by way of Arriva Kent Thameside. It moved on to Arriva Southend in 2004.

Above: Eight MCW Metrobuses were operated by Arriva in Colchester, emanating from the group's London fleets. This example, which had been converted to single-door layout, ran from 1999 to 2002.

Above: Some visitors stayed but briefly in the town, including this 1985 Leyland Olympian with ECW body, which only ran for a few months in 2002. It came from Arriva's Southend fleet but had been new to Crosville in the days of the National Bus Company.

Below: Colchester Borough Transport was a regular customer for Leyland's Lynx, but despite the Essex registration this wasn't one of CBT's own Lynxes. It had been new to County Bus of Harlow in 1990 and came to Colchester from Arriva East Herts & Essex in 2001. It was still in use when TGM took over the town's bus services but was withdrawn at the start of 2006, still in Arriva livery. This photograph was taken in 2004.

Right: After taking over from Arriva TGM applied Network Colchester fleetnames to Arriva-liveried buses, including this DAF SB220 with 48-seat Ikarus body. The DAF was much-travelled, having started life with Manchester-area operator Stuarts in 1992 and passed through the hands of three other operators before reaching Colchester. It is seen at Coddenham, Suffolk, in April 2005.

Left: TGM invested in new buses for the town. One of eight Dennis Darts that entered service in December 2004 shows the Network Colchester fleetname and the use of route branding for service 1. The 37-seat Pointer bodywork was built in Falkirk, hence the Scottish registration mark.

Right: The first new double-decker for Network Colchester was this Scania N94 with 80-seat East Lancs body. Delivered in 2005, it was indeed the first new double-decker for the fleet since 1991 and the days of Colchester Borough Transport. It operates on the Colchester–Ipswich service, previously run by First Eastern Counties.

Right: Older double-deckers have also received Network Colchester colours, including four Volvo B10Ms which had been part of the Arriva Colchester fleet from 2002. These have 88-seat East Lancs bodywork and were new in 1989 to London & Country.

Below: An older Network Colchester Dart, with 40-seat East Lancs body, carries branding for service 5. New in 1995, the bus had been transferred to Arriva Colchester in 2002 from Arriva Guildford & West Surrey.

Top: Network Colchester is managed from Haverhill, headquarters of fellow TGM subsidiary Burton's Coaches. Two Burton's vehicles —1998 Volvo B10Ms with Van Hool Alizée bodywork — carry Colchester Coachways fleetnames in small lettering beneath the Burton's name.

Above: The first dedicated school bus for the Network Colchester fleet arrived in January 2006. An MCW Metrobus II new to South Yorkshire PTE 20 years earlier, it had served with MK Metro, Classic Buses of Annfield Plain and then Burton's, whose name it still carried upon entering service in Colchester.

Interesting Times

The years after local bus deregulation in 1986 were arguably the most interesting in the history of the British bus industry. DAVID THROWER takes a look.

All photographs by Stewart J. Brown

"May you live in interesting times!" is reputedly an old Chinese curse. For the bus industry, and for the enthusiast, there was never a more interesting time than two decades ago, in the mid-1980s.

Back in the early decades of the 20th century a system of regulation and quantity-controlled licensing was progressively introduced, affecting every aspect of bus operation. But in the 1980s the then Conservative Government decided to sweep large chunks of it away, arguing that it was holding the industry back.

The precursor to bus deregulation, as it would come to be known, was the deregulation of long-distance coaching, with effect from 6 October 1980. This had attracted relatively little attention outside the immediate industry and was introduced without public controversy. After all, few of the chattering classes actually used coaches, and, on the face of it, there seemed to be relatively little to argue about. And new players in the express coach industry, such as Stagecoach, would offer greater customer choice, including additional routes and lower fares. All to the good.

The decline in local bus use, of course, had been extremely severe, stretching right back to the early 1950s in affluent areas and to the 1960s in the less affluent industrial towns. Decline was due partly to factors that were outside the industry's control — growing affluence inevitably meant an increase in car ownership, and the consequent road congestion was the responsibility of highway engineers who invariably seemed to have the needs of private motorists — including themselves — uppermost in mind.

But there were aspects for which the industry itself was directly to blame. Poor labour relations, strikes and wasteful practices were compounded by bureaucratic controls, a lack of imagination and a conservative (with a small 'c') outlook. In some cases wage settlements were excessive and were granted by union-influenced local authorities which seemed happy to buy peace at any price, even if it meant yet another round of fares increases and service cuts.

A new beginning

The architects of bus deregulation were those within the industry who saw a chance to try to break out of this endless vicious circle of decline.

In many ways, it was a very brave attempt to try to reassert management's right to manage, to introduce greater efficiencies and to reduce or eliminate cross-subsidy between profitable and unprofitable routes. On this latter point analysts felt that passengers were being deterred from busy routes by excessively high fares that had been introduced solely to prop up other loss-making services elsewhere in the network. Removing cross-subsidy would enable passengers to be won back on these busy routes through sharp fare reductions, even if a few passengers were lost from consequential cuts to unremunerative services. There was much to commend this approach.

The Government also wanted to break up and sell off publicly-owned bus operations. It saw public ownership as a part-cause of the industry's stagnation, lacking the profit motivation; municipal and Passenger Transport Executive operators were furthermore seen as part of 'municipal socialism'. There was also genuine concern that big was not beautiful. Even non-municipal and shire-county operations were large and unwieldy. For instance, in the mid-1980s the National Bus Company had no fewer than 50,000 employees and 14,000 vehicles.

The Government was also committed to reducing the power of the Transport & General Workers' Union, whose effect upon bus services was seen to be malign, due to restrictive practices and supposedly excessive wage demands. And so, the thinking went, extending deregulation to local bus services would simultaneously stop the rot, in terms of the steady decline in bus use, and spike the TGWU.

Above all there was a desire, both politically and by academic observers, as well as by some within the industry itself, to introduce new ideas. A central part of this philosophy was that, if there was a demand for a bus service between A and B, then any operator should be entitled to run any number of buses, at any times, and at any fare, just as there could be

any number of greengrocers in the high street or road hauliers on the roads. Considerable hope was expressed that taxi operators and the haulage industry might start up bus or taxi-bus services to challenge existing bus operators.

The Secretary of State for Transport of the time was Nicholas Ridley. He offered a willing ear to the advisers who were trying to bring change. The result was the 1985 Transport Act, the contents of which became public that January. This had been preceded by a White Paper, published in July 1984, which had met with intense hostility from local authorities. Usually, in such circumstances, governments would back off a few notches, and a toned-down policy would appear in the final Bill presented to Parliament for approval. But Ridley was made of sterner stuff. His view was that the drawbacks of deregulation were being hyped, whilst the benefits were being underestimated. There was, therefore, no hint of compromise, and despite widespread protests — and to the dismay of much of local government — the final Bill was virtually identical to the White Paper and was promptly steamrollered through both Houses of Parliament, few of whose occupants ever regularly sat on a bus outside London.

Introduction of bus deregulation was briefly preceded by some small trial areas, including Hereford. These appeared to have been carefully chosen so as to avoid any risk of chaos — no-one suggested Newcastle upon Tyne or Bristol as a trial area — so there was no proper opportunity to put to the test the fears of sceptics about free-for-alls in large cities. These included deep concern within the PTE areas that bus

deregulation would bring chaos — bus jams, buses jostling for passengers, shoddy buses and a lack of services on quieter routes and at quiet times on even busy routes — and threaten carefully integrated bus/rail transport, notably the Tyneside Metro.

D-Day approaches

Despite the lack of any major urban pilot schemes the Government pressed ahead with Ridley's 'big bang' approach. The date for bus deregulation outside London was set as 26 October 1986, to coincide with school half-term holidays. Services starting in October had to be pre-registered with Traffic Commissioners and local authorities — which would then identify service gaps — by 28 February 1986. In fact, Scottish operators saw little merit in waiting any longer than was necessary, having already registered all their services by mid-1986, so competition in Glasgow in particular came prematurely, at the end of August, despite resistance to deregulation within the Scottish Office.

One effect widely attributed to deregulation but which in fact pre-dated it was the introduction of local minibus networks. An initial network in Exeter was followed in mid-1985 by the conversion of Badgerline services in Weston-super-Mare, under the MiniLink name. The conventional bus service there was cut back and replaced by bright little vehicles operating on 10-minute headways. This was followed by a similar network in Oxford. However, an earlier attempt by an enterprise named AMOS to introduce such services to London was rejected — a first sign that London was a special case, and was not going to feature in the early stages of deregulation (or even at all).

Interestingly, as early as autumn 1985 the new glitz of minibus operations was already under question. Minibuses were costing just £19,000 at this time but offered only about 16-20 seats, whilst full-size double-deckers were costing about £61,000 for around 75 seats. But a minibus was reckoned to have a life of only five years, whereas a full-size bus could be expected to last 15-20 years, meaning that the whole-life operating cost per seat was very much cheaper for a heavyweight bus, even allowing for heavier maintenance costs in later life.

Not all minibuses attracted the 'cheap and nasty' tag. An outstandingly stylish design, the CityPacer, was produced by Optare. Northern Counties produced some very acceptable products on Dodge chassis, and other good-quality products appeared, such as the MCW Metrorider. But many designs, such as the Mercedes L608D, whilst they might have been more robust than Transits or Sherpas, had a downmarket 'welfare' or van image about them — hardly suitable for

tempting people out of their ever-more-refined cars. Was this the bright new dawn the travelling public were being promised? To some observers it looked more like the sort of bus operations one might see in the poorer parts of the developing world.

Second-hand big buses were also clearly going to play a major role. Most notable in 1985/6 was the introduction in Scotland of many ex-London Routemasters, which were bought cheaply, given smart repaints and pressed into service. Clydeside Scottish took 46, Kelvin Scottish 69 and Strathtay Scottish 20. Newly created companies such as Clydeside Scottish and Kelvin Scottish, formed in 1985 from bigger Scottish Bus Group subsidiaries, were joined by Stagecoach, trading as Magicbus. The enthusiasts loved the Routemasters — but open-platform buses, and in the Scottish winter?

Glasgow was also to be the first hint that a complete free-for-all might not be everything that was needed to

Below: One of the strangest happenings in the early days of deregulation was the appearance of ex-London Routemasters with operators around Britain. They were particularly popular in Scotland, being bought by the Scottish Bus Group for operation in Glasgow, Perth and Dundee. This is a Strathtay Scottish bus in Dundee.

Above: Citibus started operating in Manchester in advance of deregulation, with a fleet of Leyland Panthers. This Pennine-bodied bus had been new to Preston Corporation.

improve bus travel. At the start of September 1986, still some weeks before the effects of deregulation reached England and Wales, Glasgow's Argyle Street witnessed an unprecedented bus jam, with buses taking 10 minutes to move 100 yards. The national media began to show signs of interest.

Later, numerous operators in England also tried batches of Routemasters. It was all jolly good fun for the observer (the author recalls travelling across Manchester in an elderly Bedford VAL coach, complete with conductor!), but it was hardly to be public transport's new dawn. At times it would look like anarchy.

PTE problems

In an upheaval such as bus deregulation there would inevitably be some transitional problems. But in some areas these were much greater than the advocates of deregulation had anticipated, due to what was widely seen as excessive haste by Ridley. Indeed, bus services in some of the big cities descended into near-chaos.

Nowhere were the difficulties greater than in Manchester. By the middle of 1986 the major operator, Greater Manchester Buses (formerly Greater

Manchester Transport) had registered some 320 services, covering a little over 70% of the former PTE network. A further 40 operators, many of them very small concerns, registered a further 120 routes, though some of these were only school workings or were very infrequent.

An administrative nightmare ensued for the PTE, as it struggled to identify what was still unregistered of the former network and which uneconomic routes (and uneconomic journeys on economic routes) it should subsidise as socially desirable. It then had to put these out to tender and award contracts. The intensity of the workload that this created, for the PTE, for the Traffic Commissioner, for the operators and for other organisations such as vehicle dealers, is difficult to overstate.

The key to the problem in Manchester was that Greater Manchester Buses had initially taken far too pessimistic a view as to how much existing mileage could be run commercially. This had several immediate effects. Firstly, it very unwisely left the door open for an influx of low-budget and often inexperienced and poorly financed new operators to move into the market and register some of the residue. These operators, in turn, had only months (sometimes barely weeks) to get their act together, register commercial journeys, bid for subsidised ones and try to assemble an operating base and the drivers and vehicles to deliver the services. Some of these operations, lacking reliable vehicles, decent premises and operating experience, therefore faced a steep learning curve, though most tried very hard to deliver their services.

Much more importantly, the uncertainty as to how much of the network would survive deregulation placed the PTE, as funder of loss-making services, in a very difficult position. It found itself faced with having to pay for tendered services not only on Sundays and on quiet routes in rural areas but also during evenings and even during the daytime on some mainstream routes. With little experience and without a mature market it had little clear idea of exactly how much of a subsidised network it could afford. A sort of 'sandwich' network ensued, one slice of the bread being provided by the commercial operators, the other slice by the Passenger Transport Executive, with the risk that there would be insufficient money left to pay for the jam in the middle — services that were actually quite well used, and not in remote areas, but which were not being picked up either by the main operator (or the new competitors) or by the subsidised network.

Gradually experience was gained. Operators became more prepared to register marginally unremunerative services as 'commercial', to try to keep out competitors. The PTE found out that in practice it had sufficient finance to fund additional services, because operators were submitting very keenly priced tenders. But this process took time, resulting in a deeply damaging autumn of lost services, upheaval, new operators and newly registered services. Hundreds of PTE drivers had been made redundant, yet in the first weeks of deregulation cancellations due to driver shortages were so acute that recruiting had to

start immediately after D-Day. This was the price that was paid for the Government's 'big bang' approach.

The problems were replicated in Merseyside and to a lesser extent in other large cities. The initial instability also unhappily coincided with the long dark evenings and the late-autumn poor weather — a silly mistake that could easily have been foreseen and avoided.

There were also steep fare rises. In Merseyside North Western put its fares up by 52% and abolished child fares altogether. In Sheffield, where fares had been frozen for many years, they were increased by no less than 250%, with a consequent slump in patronage of almost a quarter.

Less urban parts of the UK saw a much smoother transition than the big conurbations. This suggests that the Government would have been prudent to exclude the big cities and PTEs from deregulation's first phase whilst greater practical knowledge of its effects was gained and whilst any necessary fare rises were implemented more carefully.

Vehicle variety

The effect upon the quality of buses themselves was also very mixed and often negative, as many of the newly formed operators were using decidedly tired vehicles. Again using Greater Manchester to illustrate the point, by 1987 the streets of Manchester were being plied by buses acquired from Cambus, Cumberland, East Kent, Eastern Scottish, Grampian, Great Yarmouth, the Isle of Man, London Transport, Midland Red, Oxford-South Midland, Preston, Trent, United Counties, West Midlands PTE, Western

Left: **Coach operator Shearings started operating bus services in the Manchester area, quickly graduating from second-hand Leyland Nationals to new Tigers and then Lynxes. The Tigers had Alexander (Belfast) bodies, unusual on this side of the Irish Sea. This one is seen in a street in central Manchester which no longer exists, having been covered over by a revitalised and expanded Arndale Centre. The photograph was taken after Shearings sold its bus operations to Timeline, which retained the Shearings livery.**

National and West Yorkshire PTE, to name but some. This, of course, raised the average age of the total vehicle fleet, dramatically reversed standardisation and made maintenance much more difficult. Meanwhile, ironically, some of the PTE's more modern vehicles were laid up and then sold. Closed garages filled with silent lines of withdrawn modern buses was one of the scandals of the early months of deregulation. Elsewhere there was similar turmoil; in the North East, for example, the Tyne & Wear Omnibus Co filled Newcastle with ageing Bristols from all corners of the UK.

Another result of deregulation was the continuing invasion by minibuses. Like swarms of locusts these swept across cities such as Leicester and parts of Liverpool. Manchester again featured, new operator United Transport International, trading as Bee Line, commencing operation with more than 200 lightweight minibuses, mainly Carlyle-bodied Freight Rover Sherpas. Greater Manchester Buses responded with a similar-sized fleet of slightly bigger Dodge/Northern Counties minibuses branded 'Little Gem' (*i.e.* 'Little GM'). Some suburban routes saw immense increases in frequency — the sight of a lightly loaded Atlantean at traffic lights was replaced by that of a long queue of virtually empty minibuses — but the patronage simply couldn't sustain this madness. Within a year or so, many of the services had vanished again, forever. By mid-1988 Bee Line was in difficulties, a victim of its

Above: Deregulation really did introduce unusual vehicles to local bus services, as demonstrated by this ECW-bodied Leyland Leopard operated by Stuarts of Hyde. At least it sported proper destination displays. A reminder of more stable days is provided by the GM Buses Metrobus in the background.

own promises, and would eventually be bought out by one of its competitors.

The van-derived minibuses also couldn't withstand the start-stop hammering of suburban bus operations. They were cramped, noisy and lacked basics such as adequate luggage space. Their lives were brutally short, and by the early 1990s they were a rarity on city services.

Although the minibus revolution was good news for the light-van industry, their use — and that of second- or third-hand heavyweight buses such as Bristol REs — had a devastating effect upon the traditional bus-manufacturing industry, which found itself with virtually no orders. Leyland saw orders fall by two thirds between 1985 and 1987.

The upheaval of deregulation in cities such as Manchester and Sheffield did immense damage to patronage. In Manchester the steady decline in ridership had been halted by 1985, through the combination of a three-year fares freeze and other marketing initiatives. Following deregulation patronage

Left: One of the smallest newcomers in Greater Manchester was the Atherton Bus Company, running between Bolton and Atherton. Its regular bus was this Alexander-bodied Leyland Atlantean, which had been new to the Greater Glasgow PTE. Note the route branding on the side.

Right: Perhaps the ultimate irony was when a major operator faced competition from a newcomer using the major operator's cast-off buses. Stotts of Oldham ran this ex-Greater Manchester Fleetline in competition with its former owner.

Left: The Bee Line Buzz Company started running minibuses in Manchester 1987 but threw in the towel after just over 18 months, selling out to Ribble, at that time an independent business. Its new owner soon abandoned the high ideals of Bee Line, replacing modern minibuses with elderly double-deckers, such as this ECW-bodied Leyland Atlantean which had been new to Ribble.

Top: Many established operators responded to competition by setting up low-cost operating units with elderly vehicles and with staff employed on less favourable conditions. Busways revived Newcastle Corporation's pre-1950 livery with the fleetname Blue Bus Services. This Bristol RE had been new to Colchester Corporation.

Above: Kinch was a highly respected Leicestershire coach operator which diversified into bus operation. Elderly used buses were not always totally reliable, as demonstrated by a Kinch Leyland National being attended by the company's breakdown truck in Loughborough.

slumped, private-car use soared, and immense damage was inflicted on public transport's credibility as an alternative to the car. The story was repeated in South and West Yorkshire, Tyneside and the West Midlands and in many other large cities. Some of the lost traffic later returned, but much did not. This was not a judgement upon bus deregulation as a philosophy but was a severe indictment of the way in which it was implemented.

One of the more bizarre aspects of deregulation was that operators had to register agreements with other operators, so as to reduce the risk of secret deals and anti-competitive pacts. This meant that it was henceforth very difficult for two operators, each providing two buses an hour along a route, to arrange these so that a balanced 15-minute service could be provided. Instead, there was a temptation for each operator to try to beat the other, to scoop the queue — all very exciting, but pointless, as it meant that buses would then arrive in pairs, followed by lengthy gaps. Once again the winners were the private car, the taxi and the moped.

In a few instances on-street competition bordered on the lawless. In Blackpool competition between new operator Easyway and municipal Blackpool Transport

led to a BT inspector and a service vehicle being shunted aside by buses of Easyway, whose proprietor had to be removed four times by the police after lying down in the road in front of his rival's buses.

Much effort by operators was misdirected at giving each other a black eye instead of getting on with the job of providing reliable services. Again, northwest England seemed to be a hotbed for such antics: Greater Manchester Buses launched an ill-starred invasion of the Blackburn area, while Merseybus poured vehicles into East Manchester, prompting GME to mount counter-invasions of the Wirral. Such ventures were usually short-lived but created much confusion among passengers — and work for staff — without significantly increasing bus use overall.

Below: Londoners could be forgiven for not recognising the setting for this view of a London Northern Ailsa outside the Bond Street Centre, which is stretching the concept of North London just a bit. The location is Leeds, and the bus, running for an unidentified operator, is heading for Castleford. Scenes like this were not uncommon in the confused days of the late 1980s and early 1990s. The Alexander-bodied Ailsa had started life with West Midlands PTE.

Above: In 1993 war broke out between the two former PTE-owned businesses in the North West of England. Birkenhead & District might have looked like yet another upstart small operator with big ideas but was in fact the name used by GM Buses North for its brief incursion to the Wirral Peninsula. This is a Northern Counties-bodied Daimler Fleetline in central Liverpool.

Below: MTL Manchester was the Merseyside PTE's bus-operating company's incursion into Greater Manchester. This is an East Lancs-bodied Atlantean.

Top and above: In the North East of England Classic Coaches competed with Go-Ahead Northern, as shown by this Leyland National in Newcastle with Classicliner branding. Northern responded with a red Superliner livery which was a passable imitation of Classic's, as demonstrated by this ECW-bodied Olympian.

rder

Gradually a degree of order emerged out of the chaos. By the late 1980s the large number of new low-cost operators was helping to keep down tender prices, while established operators found that it was sometimes tactically advantageous to register even loss-making services as 'commercial', as a means of preventing new operators from gaining a foothold. This brought cross-subsidy back into fashion, but for few reasons.

Meanwhile the smart money was being made by companies such as Brian Souter's Stagecoach, which quietly made millions by buying up former National Bus Company subsidiaries, selling off valuable assets such as bus-station and bus-garage sites and introducing modern buses operating from industrial estates and new small outstation bases.

By the end of the 1980s the number of new service registrations in each Traffic Commissioner's area had calmed down to much more manageable proportions, and the industry at last started to get its breath back. Quite a few new operators had gone to the wall, and many others had been taken over. The early 1990s were to continue this process of merger and takeover.

London had meanwhile remained as an island of regulation. It is hard to avoid the conclusion that Ridley and his successors lost their nerve in London's case,

fearing log-jams of tatty DMSs, second-hand provincial Atlanteans and cheap minibuses on their doorstep in Whitehall and daily gridlock in Oxford Street. Had such events occurred there would have been uproar in the London-centric media, with a heavy political price to pay.

Thus, almost by default, a very different approach developed in the capital. Huge economies were made in London's bus operations. Aldenham Works closed in 1986, followed by Chiswick Works, and even Bus Engineering Ltd, which was sold off to the private sector and moved to Willesden, did not survive long. More and more bus services were contracted out. Most suburban routes lost their Routemasters and with them their conductors. Backroom offices closed, administration was decentralised, and there were significant redundancies among white-collar staff.

Instead of unfettered competition London got route

Below: Many of the new operators of local bus services in the 1980s were ultimately absorbed by established operators. That was the fate of Your Bus, which competed with West Midlands Travel in south Birmingham. This Plaxton-bodied Leyland Tiger retains Your Bus livery, but the WM Your Bus sticker below the windscreen shows who's really in charge.

Left: In the late 1980s Liverpool attracted a number of new operators the most prominent of which were Fareway, Liverline and Liverbus. All were relatively short-lived. Liverline, which started operations in 1988, was bought in 1993 by British Bus, which initially retained the company's name, as seen on this Park Royal-bodied Atlantean which had been new to London Country. The blue livery is a British Bus adaptation of Liverline's colour scheme.

Left: Fareway started off in 1986 with second-hand double-deckers but was soon buying new vehicles. The first were long-wheelbase Leyland Olympians with Northern Counties bodywork. Fareway was taken over by Merseyside Transport in 1993, by which time it ran almost 70 buses.

Left: OK was an old-established independent which expanded rapidly after deregulation, buying both new and used buses. The new vehicles included relatively rare Volvo B6s with Plaxton Pointer bodywork.

Above: **The emerging new groups frequently shuffled buses around, hence the unlikely sight of a Green Line Leyland Olympian coach leaving Newcastle for Blyth. The Olympian was operated by Northumbria and had been transferred from Kentish Bus. Both companies were part of the Proudmutual group.**

tendering, and when this started London Buses subsidiaries had a poor success rate. The very image of the London bus was challenged, most notably when Grey-Green won the contract for route 24, running right past Parliament's front door. But there was some unease at this threat to one of London's tourist trademarks, the red double-decker. Routemasters therefore remained on Central London services, and, gradually, London Buses subsidiaries found their feet and won more franchises.

The message was clear: slim down, or see your routes lost to outsiders, your staff out of a job and your garages close. The lessons were rapidly learned, but many long-established London bus garages still fell victim to closure.

Although minibuses were introduced in significant numbers in the suburbs, there were very few minibus operations tried in the centre of London. Reluctantly the Government had to acknowledge that London was a special case, and it remains regulated to this day.

Retrospect

So, in retrospect, what are we to make of those turbulent few years between 1986 and 1989? It wasn't fully realised by enthusiasts at the time, but we undoubtedly witnessed the most remarkable period in British bus history. Roads that had never seen a service found themselves with 20 buses an hour, even if they were only minibuses. There were Routemasters

in Poole and Perth, Western National DMSs in Manchester, Bristol REs everywhere, and some oddity or other in pretty well every town outside London. Services changed every few weeks, or so it seemed.

Operators seemed to think that the enemy was the other operators, instead of the private car. Car sales and use soared. Where there was chaos people took lifts, moved house, changed jobs, bought mopeds, got out the push-bike, switched to rail … anything to avoid using buses.

For the enthusiast it was, briefly, a field-day. No-one knew it at the time, but the bus scene of 1996-9 would look very different indeed from that of 1986-9 — and, for the enthusiast, much more dull. A unique era had passed, almost in a flash, and those who had not sampled it (and photographed it) had missed their chance for ever. Almost before we knew it, it was over, and the scrapyards were brimming with Clydeside Routemasters, Ford Transit-based minibuses and fourth-hand Bristols.

The litmus test of bus deregulation is patronage.

Above: A bit of sabre-rattling by Badgerline saw the company set up Frontline Buses in 1993 to compete with British Bus subsidiary Midland Red North. The small Frontline fleet included this Leyland Leopard which had been rebodied by Willowbrook. Note the badger behind the rear wheel. Frontline was sold to British Bus in 1995.

Did it stop the rot and stem the seemingly inexorable decline in bus use across the UK?

The answer, as is so often the case, was that the initial years of deregulation were a hotch-potch of missed opportunities, optimistic new services, upheaval and chaos (in some cities), long-overdue streamlining of costs, plus a few innovative ideas. It wasn't an across-the-nation disaster, but neither was it an unqualified success. If one could make a generalisation, this would be that it helped bus travel in small towns and rural areas, and muddled it up in the large cities. The Government of the time claimed an early success. Deregulation's opponents slammed it as a disaster. In truth, both were largely wrong.

In one respect, bus deregulation was outstanding. It achieved its objective of breaking the trade unions. On 26 October 1986 the TGWU saw decades of hard-won concessions go out the door in a single night. The new order meant lower wages, longer hours, more intensive scheduling, fewer perks and a much less tolerant attitude to clowning about. The Reg Varney image of bus crews was brought to an abrupt end. Days lost to

strikes were greatly reduced, and sickness and absenteeism fell markedly. Many left the industry, and those who stayed felt the job had lost its soul, but the bus industry became much better focussed upon the needs of customers who in the past had sometimes come a poor third, after the management and the unions.

Will re-regulation ever occur outside London? Only time will tell, but, despite repeated calls for at least a partial return to the pre-1986 scenario, particularly in the large metropolitan areas, scrapping of the 1985 Act's main provisions seems unlikely. We will probably have to make do with what we have, for the foreseeable future, with the underlying demand for buses propped up by pro-public transport policies and funded by grants from central government, and with quality being controlled by tendering authorities, annual vehicle inspections and the various safety bodies.

But the sharp disparity between the London and out-of-London systems remains as a nagging judgement upon Ridley and his advisers. Between 2000/1 and 2004/5 bus use in franchised, regulated London climbed a further 32%, whereas across the rest of deregulated England during the same period it fell by 6%, though interestingly Scotland and Wales managed a small (3%) increase. Such sustained growth in London and continuing decline in the remainder of England will continue to pose uncomfortable questions as to whether or not deregulation, particularly in the major conurbations, was the salvation for bus travel that its exponents claimed.

The Potsdam Dutchmen

ROBERT E. JOWITT, not without risk to life and limb, explores with many fond memories the Benelux transport he had not seen for some four decades ... with just a few of the memories still proving intact!

All photographs by the author

nce upon a time, close on half a century ago, I found a magic city. In a few square miles — or kilometres — surrounded by gracious steep hills made by God and equally steep but perhaps less attractive slag heaps made by man, this fairytale domain boasted three separate if intermingled tram systems on two different gauges and also two trolleybus outfits, the one with some of its vehicles so archaic that they had their trolley booms mounted one above the other instead of side-by-side as modern practice demanded, and the other with trolleybuses which had once been double-ended on three equidistantly-spaced axles ... though by the time I arrived wiser counsels had prevailed and while still on three axles they were driveable only from one end.

And just a few miles of bus journey away, at Poulseur, a steam tram flourished, albeit hauling only goods trains.

The hub of this paradisiacal empire was a square known as Place St Lambert, where a double circle of tram tracks and crossovers and junctions was laid out in its entirety in both metre-gauge and standard-gauge, with trolleybus overhead *tant bien que mal* (or more or less) to match, the complete set-up being described in local or vulgar parlance as *Le Tramodrome*.

The city was called Liège, in a country called Belgium.

I heard of it first through an intrepid British explorer of far-away places where British bus enthusiasts would not care to visit or indeed to be seen dead (which quite possibly was how they thought they might end up — an attitude towards which I have recently had occasion to feel some sympathy, as I shall in due time reveal), the explorer being the renowned John C. Gillham.

Liège and indeed Belgium still exist, but the transport of Liège as I knew it must seem now almost mythical, though it was real enough at the time for me to drag my early-1960s girlfriend Carol there through frost and snow to prove its truth, and in point of fact my efforts both literary and photographically at recording it have been reproduced in a fairly serious volume, published in the city itself, relating such pursuits.

Left: Jowitt's 1959 view of the Liège Tramodrome, with metre-gauge SNCV car on the left and standard-gauge Liège tram right.

And while I was engaged in my first foray on photographing the *Tramodrome* in the summer of 1959 I happened to catch sight of another chap apparently engaged upon the same business. So I said to him, in good round English: "Are you photographing the trams?" He told me, much later, that he was amazed firstly that I should speak to him at all, and secondly, in the streets of a city where either French or Flemish must prevail, that I should tackle him in English. He admitted on the spot, however, that my accusation on tramway photography was accurate.

Now at that date I was much involved with pen-friends (this, long before internet or similar evil devices, being regarded as a respectable form of international communication spreading world-wide goodwill and fellowship, etc), even if most of my pen-friends were German girls who stuck President Heuss stamps at unlikely angles on various corners of their envelopes (much, I must suppose, to the irritation of the postal employees who had to postmark the stamps) to indicate various degrees of passion, none of which was ever fulfilled, and, being aware of the potential short-falling of the maids of Westfalen, I thought I might turn the pen-friendship notion to better advantage.

Thus; "I'll give you my address and you give me yours, and we can send each other photographs of trams." His name was, and still is, Gerrit-Jan, at that date of Utrecht but now of Rotterdam.

This excellent Dutchman is, so far as I am aware, the only person alive, apart from my darling sister (my parents being now long since gathered on another shore) who can claim to have known my first best beloved girlfriend and my three subsequent wives. Moreover, in the four subsequent decades, be it sporadically, Gerrit-Jan and I have continued to send each other tramway photographs, or items of news on narrow-gauge travel, and once or twice he has come over to GB, *en route* to do some ballast-shovelling on the Ffestiniog, to inspect what I am doing in the preservation of 1930s Parisian buses.

Meanwhile, in 1966, my then wife and I launched a photographic attack, partly under the auspices of Gerrit-Jan, on the tramways of Belgium and the Netherlands, and this was the last time, until the episodes which I will describe hereinafter, that I had any encounter with the Low Countries.

In the course of this 1966 visit Gerrit-Jan's father, while we supped at their table, elected to recite, or almost to sing, a verse alleged to come from British troops engaged in the Netherlands in the Napoleonic wars and who, naturally ignorant of whence came their foes, would chant: *'The Rotterdam Dutchmen, the Amsterdam Dutchmen, the Potsdam Dutchmen, and all the Dam Dutchmen!'* Thus to this day I can never think of the inhabitants of Benelux except as Potsdam

Dutchmen.

Meanwhile again, in 1970, my darling sister elected to be married, and chose as wedding-day transport my newly-acquired 1935 Renault Paris bus, and on this joyful occasion (I hardly dare say at this juncture that my darling sister's name is Joy!) there was a bridesmaid, a chum of Joy's from a local church youth group, by name Helen.

Meanwhile again, Gerrit-Jan, possibly inspired either by something I had said in Liège or something I had written in some letter thereafter, was setting out to establish a model railway track, though all I could claim in the field was Hornby or Basset-Lowke clockwork.

And meanwhile, yet again, I had embarked on a career as a tramway photographer, and in due time acquired some (ill?) repute in this field.

While back in Rotterdam the good Gerrit-Jan was proceeding with his model railway and tramway, with a complexity of gauges close approaching those of the Liège *Tramodrome*, and *la belle* Helen, apart from becoming a wife and mother and then an invaluable translator for boring EEC documents in Luxembourg, spent considerable time in typing out in legible form on computer my mother's memoirs or autobiography, she (Helen) being a great admirer of her (my mother) … and Gerrit-Jan presented me with two huge volumes of photographs of the model-railway layout as completed after three decades of work, while Helen signally failed to provide me with a printed-out copy of my mother's words, due merely to her (Helen's) inability ever to submit paper to post.

The only solution, after lengthy telephone calls, was to go and collect my mother's memoirs from Helen's doorstep, and, seeing that Rotterdam and Luxembourg are geographically not so very far apart, to inspect in reality this model railway of which I had heard so much … and to examine what had befallen the tramways which I had last seen 30 or more years ago.

Thus herewith, after this long-drawn-out preamble, I will endeavour to set down my experiences, in May 2005, in search of lost youth and lost trams.

Just to start these traveller's tales in the proper spirit let me say I left my Isle of Wight home by Southern Vectis and hasty change onto WightBus rail-link (simply to prove I am a bona-fide bus passenger, not a motorist) and ended up catching Eurostar. I could not bring myself to admire this — too soulless compared with the inconvenient romance of a Dover–Ostend packet boat in the summer of 1959, when by good fortune I was the only English boy in a party of 40 *Fräulein* — but must admit to its being a speedy way of reaching Brussels and, with change of train, Rotterdam not too long afterwards.

The Rotterdam Dutchman and I then spent the next few days, when not engaged upon his model railway, n pursuit of trams in Rotterdam, Amsterdam and Den Haag. I had been well aware, four decades before, that the cars and the practices on these three systems were completely individual and, despite geographical and national proximity, bore no resemblance one to another, and now, even though all I remembered was utterly departed — save once one of those magnificent RET central-entrance bogie-cars, today a preserved specimen, rumbling down the Coolsingel and once a Den Haag PCC which I had known as brand-new slinking past the Buitenhof as converted to a works-car — the differences between the three systems, even in modernity, remained as manifest as before.

I felt it only tactful, as Gerrit-Jan is an ardent devotee of electric traction and hardly at all in favour of buses except as a desirable alternative to private cars, to be somewhat circumspect in my efforts at photographing the buses, delectable though many of these proved to me … more especially the articulated buses which, particularly in Amsterdam, bounded over humped-back bridges in splendid camel-style. Though of course the humped-back bridge approach is even more sensational when attacked by a five-section articulated tram.

Naturally, given my feelings for trams — or buses — based entirely on their aesthetic merit backed sometimes by their architectural background or by a foreground of young ladies such as I can never ignore, I entertained no knowledge of the dates or makes of such transports as passed before my eyes.

I might add that the architecture in Amsterdam was much as I remembered it, whereas in Den Haag (though the old bits remained the same) and in Rotterdam the skyscrapers had shot up, and indeed impressively, and the public transport beneath had grown to match …

I moved on, or back, to Antwerp, to meet with bridesmaid Helen, who had some commitment there, and we had pre-arranged this meeting for her to drive me back to Luxembourg to collect my mother's autobiography. We sat at a pavement café table sampling diverse Belgian beers (well, I did, but she less so, naturally, as she was driving) and watching the trams. In my youth the trams were all classic four-wheelers (apart, of course, from SNCV trams) but in a later visit, in 1966, the Belgian PCC had interrupted. Incredibly, nearly 40 years on, many of these were still surviving, but I have to admit that the replacing up-to-date five-section-articulateds serve artistically more impressively than even double-coupled old PCCs on the tortuous twists in the ancient narrow streets.

Nevertheless the PCCs were definitely a case of *à la recherche des temps perdus*. Thus I didn't pay much attention to Antwerp buses … give or take a few in the incredible tree-clad bus-station.

Then Helen motored me off to Luxembourg, via various *autoroutes* and a splendid sunset over the summits of the Ardennes.

I had asked Helen to try to obtain for me the local and inter-urban bus timetables. She hadn't, but handed me my mother's memoirs instead. This much achieved, I visited the enquiry office at *La Gare*, and was presented with a volume almost biblical in proportions for the city routes, and a derisive slap of the hand on

Below: Amsterdam four-axle articulated buses in August 1959. Note the letterbox to the fore.

Left: Architectural splendours — royal palace to the right, post office behind a Berkhof-bodied artic — in Amsterdam.

Right: Getting the hump in Amsterdam, May 2005.

Left: Modernity in Rotterdam trams, with a five-section articulated unit.

Right: The elegantly tree-clad and adequately shelter-provided bus station in Antwerp is the terminus for yellow-striped buses of De Lijn.

Above: Curvaceous Antwerp modernity, May 2005.

the part of the inspector over something like two quires or whatever of about 1,000 sheets of A4 and, effectively, "Those are the interurban bus timetables and you can't have 'em!" (All in most polite Luxembourg French.) "Where do you want to go?" I had no idea where I wanted to go and, with some relief that Helen had never tried to fulfil my request, I went outside *La Gare* and witnessed the truth.

On one side and another of the station — which boasted scale and architectural design closely approximating an Austrian or Eastern Swiss cathedral — were bus stops, three or four beside each other, constantly filled with departures of Luxembourg city buses, either normal or not infrequently articulated, or diverse and several rural or interurban operators, with monsters, mostly, so far as I could observe, attributable to MAN or Mercedes — and it afforded me some pleasure, I must admit, to observe that bus-manufacturing names from my youth were still extant — which were, on their three axles, 15 metres in length (as I have been told since by a reliable authority who also described them as the poor operator's version of the artic!) and, in a variety of far from unattractive liveries, proved some of the most impressive buses I have ever beheld. After all, learning to love, as a teenager, those glorious French three-axle Berliets which were actually less than 12 metres long, this new vision was surely an eye-opener!

Even greater than these, however, was definitely the double-decker version of the same! I saw it but twice. Once, when from a distance I was photographing the

noble Pont Alphonse and the creature crossed it, and once again when, thoroughly luggage laden, on a bus hastening for a train, I caught a glimpse of it down a side street and, under such circumstances, impossible to hark back to chase it …

My other disaster in Luxembourg was that at something like 17.00hrs, when, as I became all too conscious, every bus from *La Gare* set out on its journey, I was stuck in an un-photogenic position behind some scaffolding, and by the time I had extricated myself from this impasse the tide had passed and I had lost a dozen or more buses storming furiously ahead in line. *Merde!* — as the French, apparently very rudely, curse.

I must not, however, complain too much. With my Benelux rail-pass, and in the intervals of Luxembourg joys, I took a day trip to Brussels, over the utterly charming railway through the Ardennes. In Brussels I started at La Bourse, which as I remembered had been glad with every sort of Brussels tram but now proved entirely bereft. (I think they were all by now underground, whither I was not prepared to explore.)

As, however, the architecture of La Bourse remained as splendid as ever, I tried to teach myself in the art of up-to-date buses as a photographic substitute. And then I trekked up towards the Palais de Justice, and hereabouts encountered numerous trams of the modern ilk and a few PCC-related examples of the modernity I had not admired 30 years before … and several quite delightful articulated buses … though I know not what of such breed they may be.

On my last departure from Luxembourg I elected to travel via Liège, thus far on a loco-hauled train with classic coaches of the early 1960s with proper opening

Above: Voyages Vandivinit operates local services in Luxembourg. This bus is on the service to Remich. Voyages Emile Weber runs across the French border to Etain.

Below: Luxembourg articulation, with a Neoplan approaching and an MAN departing.

Left: Luxembourg city livery on Mercedes Citaro artic.

Below: A 15m MAN in Luxembourg, part of the two-dozen-strong La Fraise fleet.

Left: Decorative Luxembourg Scania OmniCity.

windows through most glorious scenery … and actually passing what appeared to be the remains of the shed at Poulseur which had sheltered, in a smoky frosty dawn in my youth, the steam tram locomotive. One look at the arising Liège tide of Euro-skyscrapers having bade me firmly not to tarry or to seek for days long gone, I caught the next train for Brussels and, dumping my baggage in a locker, the next train on for Ghent.

I had not seen Ghent since the last days of its classic tramcars, when they were about to be replaced, oh, horror, by PCCs, of which case I entirely disapproved. Now — and in the same livery as the Antwerp trams, and for logistical reasons for which I can furnish no explanation save transport alterations as widespread as elsewhere — they, the PCCs, and subsequent bendi-trams, appear in the same De Lijn colours as in Antwerp and elsewhere.

Nevertheless a journey round the (sometimes hideous and less tourist-visited) circumferences of Ghent in a more-than-30-year-old PCC, even if much mutilated in the course of years, was an utter delight, going far to prove that progress, much as I deem it all too often retrograde, is not without its charms. De Lijn had some quite pretty bendibuses in Ghent too.

Ghent boasted some trolleybus wires, apparently a relatively recent introduction (and certainly not there in the old days) but no trolleybuses were to be seen. This may have been on account of roadworks or perhaps for more sinister reasons … trolleybuses in Ghent are said to prove unpopular with the populace, though I don't know why.

Another example of present bad taste (do I risk a pun?) was that the traditional Belgian tavern or restaurant in which I had dined with darling Carol in the freezing fog of the spring of 1963, with a constant passage of elderly bow-collector trams reflected in the huge mirrors on its walls, had been given over to that old Scots-sounding American with the well-stocked farm. Fortunately I wasn't hungry.

On returning to Brussels and before catching my booked Eurostar I had a couple of hours in hand, so I set out south west from the Gare du Midi, surely one of the most civilised railway stations in Europe, along the tramlines, which produced *inter alia* several specimens of original (if re-liveried) PCCs.

On my way back from this foray, including visits to most charming shopkeepers for an extra film, should I need it, and bread, cheese and wine which definitely I needed to face the Eurostar, I saw oncoming a tram

Above: If the author viewed with horror in 1966 the soon-to-be-replacement of classic trams in Ghent by PCC cars, he now views such replacements as still survive intact with the greatest delight.

in the all-over advertising livery of the Belgian equivalent of Yellow Pages. As in the vicissitudes of my career I have spent some time delivering such volumes myself I could not resist shooting this. And while I was thus engaged a car between me and the tram paused momentarily, and one of two African women inside it screeched at me "*Faites pas des photos!*", though why she should object to my attempting to photograph a *Pages d'Or* (note that they are gold, not yellow, in Belgium) tram is more than I can imagine.

At this instant a gent of east-of-eastern-Mediterranean appearance who happened to be passing by on the pavement — nothing at all, so far as I believe, to do with the girls in the car — repeated the screech "*Faites pas des photos!*" and bashed me twice, hard, in the face. Something tinkled in the gutter but, with a quick glance to see it wasn't any of my film cassettes, I started to retreat.

Rescue then appeared imminent in the form of another East-of-Suez chap who seemed as if he was about to enquire sensibly into what was happening, but he in his turn launched a savage but fortunately extremely wide-of-the-mark kick at me … and then both these gents trotted away along the pavement,

probably completely oblivious to the sport in which the moment before they had been occupied, while I, hastening the other way, realised that the tinkle in the gutter had been my glasses … luckily my spare pair; my best Armani bifocals were safe in my pocket.

I decided not to go back to look for the others; they might have been run over by now anyway. To prove to myself, nevertheless, that I was not downhearted, I managed to click off a few more trams, albeit circumspectly, between the scene of the crime and the portals of the Gare.

Once on the Eurostar I discovered that the potentially deadly kick must in fact have contacted my wine bottle. When I tried to pull the cork the whole neck of the bottle collapsed in shards of broken glass. I had to pour the wine into a plastic cup through sheets of Kleenex tissue. Very inconvenient … But really I needed the wine.

I needed to reflect. In four decades of tram or bus photography I had suffered only one other serious unpleasantness, when a brand new Bronica was slipped from my shoulder bag in a Lisbon crowd. This is not bad going. I would not be put off.

So I must return, and try to chase that double-decker … and be in the right photographic position at 5pm.

I think, however, that I won't bother with Liège, I will be content to live with magic memories; and I certainly will not again attempt to attend upon the present on the south side of Brussels Gare du Midi.

Highland Fling

Highland Omnibuses was, for most of its life, the poor relation in the Scottish Bus Group family, operating buses which were no longer needed by its more prosperous southern sister companies. STEWART J. BROWN tells the story.

With sparsely populated territory and only one major centre of population, Highland Omnibuses was always the poor relation in the Scottish Bus Group family.

For most of its life the Inverness-based company made do with elderly buses transferred from sister SBG companies, creating a fleet with interesting buses and what might be described as an interesting age profile too. Highland Omnibuses' omnibuses were often old. And sometimes very old.

Highland Omnibuses came into being in February 1952, a new company set up to combine the businesses of the Highland Transport Co and MacRae & Dick, both companies based in Inverness.

Highland Transport had been set up in 1930 to take over the operations of Inverness & District Motor Services. This followed the acquisition of a 50% stake in Inverness & District by the LMS Railway.

The railway's interest in Highland Transport passed to the new British Transport Commission in 1948, and in September 1951 the British Transport Commission assumed complete ownership of the business. It was initially managed from Edinburgh by Scottish Omnibuses.

At this time Highland Transport ran 69 buses, mainly prewar Albions, wartime Bedford OWBs and Guy Arabs; there were 34 Guys, making up almost half the fleet and including all 19 double-deckers.

Whereas Highland Transport's operations extended north to Wick and Thurso, MacRae & Dick was essentially a local business operating 27 single-deck buses and coaches in the Inverness area. These included Albions, Bedfords and Austins; as well as running buses, MacRae & Dick was the Inverness Austin dealer, with a business selling and repairing cars.

Right: The last new double-decker for Highland Transport was this Guy Arab III, with unusual full-fronted lowbridge body by Strachans, which had been an exhibit at the 1950 Commercial Motor Show in London. Alongside stands a 1956 Bristol Lodekka transferred in 1963 from Scottish Omnibuses. The Guy ran until 1970; the Lodekka until 1972.
Harry Hay

So Highland Omnibuses started life with a fleet of just under 100 buses, ranging from 20-year-old Albions through to modern Guy Arabs and Austin coaches. The average age of the fleet was 8.9 years; 69% of the vehicles owned were under 10 years old. The new company adopted the dark-maroon and cream livery which had been used by Highland Transport.

Highland Transport's fleet numbers were retained, but with the addition of prefix letters to identify chassis makes. The highest-numbered bus in the Highland Transport fleet was 100, so the vehicles acquired from MacRae & Dick were numbered from 101 upwards, again with prefix letters to identify the chassis make. The use of prefix letters echoed the practice at Scottish Omnibuses, as did the adoption of depot allocation plates, although that practice died out in the 1960s.

As soon as Highland Omnibuses was established, the Scottish Omnibuses Group expanded the business by adding to it the Inverness and Nairn operations of W. Alexander & Sons. Alexander was one of Britain's biggest bus companies, with a fleet of around 2,000 vehicles covering an area from Glasgow northwards through Fife to Aberdeenshire and then eastwards to Inverness. Highland acquired 24 buses from Alexander, all but two of them Leylands, and numbered them upwards from 150. Most were double-deckers, and these included a solitary Titan PD1 which had previously been operated by Greig of Inverness on a town service. Alexander had taken over the Greig business in 1950. The PD1 survived until 1963.

The Highland fleet now stood at 120 vehicles, of which 39 were double-deckers.

The company received its first new buses in 1952, although they weren't quite as new as they seemed, being six 30ft-long Guy Arabs with 39-seat Scottish

Omnibuses bodywork based on rebuilt and lengthened wartime chassis which had been new to London Transport. Another six followed in 1953, and six more in 1954. The extensive nature of the rebuild saw these vehicles being given new registration marks issued in Edinburgh. The longest-lived of the rebuilt Guys operated for 12 years.

With the 'new' buses came assorted used vehicles from elsewhere in the Scottish Omnibuses group. At one extreme there were four-year-old Commer Commando coaches from Alexander, at the other 18-year-old Leyland Tiger buses from Central — which, despite their age, Highland ran for four years.

More typically Highland was receiving wartime Guys, from Scottish Omnibuses, David Lawson (an Alexander subsidiary) and Western SMT. Between 1955 and 1960 almost 40 wartime Guy double-deckers headed north to Highland, many being used to transport workers building the nuclear plant at Dounreay, on the northern Caithness coast. When construction work was completed Highland provided commuter services for workers at the site.

New vehicles in the 1950s included Albion Nimbuses which while they might have seemed ideal vehicles for Highland — compact 29-seaters — proved not to be so. A demonstrator was tried in 1955, followed by six coaches with Alexander bodies in 1956. And that was the end of that. The 1956 Nimbuses were, incidentally, the first new Highland Omnibuses vehicles to be registered in Inverness.

Emphasising the company's links with Scottish Omnibuses, the next new vehicles, in 1957, were AECs, and between 1957 and 1962 Highland took delivery of 33 new Reliances and six mechanically similar Monocoaches, generally similar to vehicles being supplied to Scottish Omnibuses. Ten of the early eliveries had Park Royal bodywork; all of the others were bodied by Alexander. The last were 38-seat coaches, which featured glazed cove panels and distinctive side mouldings. These turned Alexander's attractive dual-purpose body into quite a presentable coach, albeit without the glitz of proper coach bodies as built by Duple and Plaxton. However, the bulk of the additions to the Highland fleet were still redundant vehicles from other Group fleets and included 16-year-old AEC Regals and 10-year-old Bedford coaches from Scottish Omnibuses.

In 1963 there were no new vehicles for Highland, but in sharp contrast to the antiquated Regals which had headed north from Scottish Omnibuses were a fleet of heavy-duty Guy Arab UF coaches from Western SMT. These were 11 years old and had been used on Western's Glasgow–London service. Some entered service as 30-seaters with toilet compartments, but all ended up as 35-seaters, offering generous accommodation in a body designed to hold up to 41 seats. They had centre-entrance Alexander bodies. A total of 36 were acquired (plus five similar coaches from Central SMT), making up 25% of the company's fleet in the mid-1960s. They served the company for five years. Their replacements would be lighter Arab

LUFs from Western, in 1968, the last of which was withdrawn in 1972, severing the link with Guy which had started with utility Arabs for Highland Transport in 1944.

Highland's most modern double-decker in 1963 was a Guy Arab III with striking full-fronted lowbridge bodywork by Strachans. This bus had been an exhibit at the 1950 Commercial Motor Show and featured flamboyant aluminium side mouldings, although it seemed that each time it was overhauled and repainted some of the fancy metalwork would be removed.

But more modern double-deckers were about to make an appearance, in the shape of 12 seven-year-old Bristol Lodekkas from Scottish Omnibuses. These were Highland Omnibuses' first Bristols and its first ECW bodies. Yet, to illustrate the variety which made up the Highland fleet, the next double-deck additions, in 1964, were a 1940 Leyland Titan and three 20-year-old Daimler CWA6s, transferred from Midland. To be fair, these only lasted a matter of months — although all were repainted in Highland's maroon livery.

The next significant intake of double-deckers radically modernised the Highland fleet. Both Central SMT and Western SMT were unhappy with their Albion

Left: Throughout the 1950s and into the 1960s the typical Highland double-decker was a lowbridge wartime Guy Arab, such as this 1945 bus with Weymann body, seen leaving the company's Dingwall depot. The last buses of this type — including this vehicle — survived until 1967.
Harry Hay

Left: By adding some fancy mouldings Alexander's standard dual-purpose body was transformed into quite a passable coach. This style of moulding — and the use of glazed cove panels on this type of body — was used on two batches of 38-seat AEC Reliances which entered service with Highland in 1961 and 1962. *Harry Hay*

Left: In the mid-1960s heavyweight Guy Arab UFs made up 25% of Highland's fleet. Most had centre-entrance Alexander bodywork and originated with Western SMT. *Harry Hay*

Above: **Caithness contrast. An ex-London Transport Guy with Northern Counties body stands alongside an ex-Central SMT Alexander-bodied Lowlander at Dounreay. The Guy, new in 1945, reached Highland in 1957 by way of Western SMT and was withdrawn in 1966. The 1963 Lowlander operated for Highland from 1965 to 1978.** *Harry Hay*

Lowlanders, and in 1965 Central transferred 12 two-year-old Lowlanders to Highland. These were followed in 1966 by 12 from Western. More Lowlanders were to follow, replacing the last of the former Highland Transport Arabs, along with assorted other double-deck types. Central's maroon livery was not dissimilar to Highland's, and Highland adopted the Central layout, with greater areas of cream, as it repainted the ex-Western Lowlanders.

The 1960s saw retrenchment by many small operators in the north of Scotland. Most were small family businesses with only two or three vehicles, and as they gave up Highland generally took over their services and their vehicles. This, of course, saw yet more non-standard types join the fleet, such as Albion Victors, and also saw Highland's services extending to new areas, particularly in Wester Ross. The biggest acquisitions were Newton of Dingwall (seven vehicles) in 1965 and Smith of Grantown-on-Spey (16 vehicles) in 1966.

There were major changes in Highland's new vehicle purchasing in the mid-1960s. Instead of buying what were considered heavyweight vehicles by the standards of the day — AEC Reliances — Highland switched to lightweights. In 1964 it took eight Bedford VAS buses, followed by two more in 1965. A bigger VAM followed in 1966, with a unique Alexander Y-type

body with 24 seats and a large mail compartment. This was, incidentally, the first Y type in the Highland fleet and was an exhibit at the 1965 Scottish Motor Show in Glasgow's Kelvin Hall.

Along with the VAM in 1966 came two Ford R-series — the first new Fords for a Scottish Bus Group fleet. These came from the stock of Millburn Motors, the Glasgow Ford coach dealer, one having a Duple Midland bus body, the other being a Plaxton coach. Earlier in the year Millburn had supplied Highland with a pair of two-year-old Ford/Duple coaches — unusual purchases in themselves, as it was rare for SBG to take in second-hand vehicles from outside the Group. One of these had been new to Happiways Tours of Manchester and was delivered in that operator's blue and grey livery, which Highland adopted as a new standard for its coach fleet. This was applied to selected existing vehicles, as well as to new purchases from 1966 onwards.

Other vehicles to come to Highland from outside the Group were six Guy Arab UFs with Duple coach bodywork from Welsh operator Red & White and six all-Leyland Royal Tiger buses from Ribble. These joined the Highland fleet in 1967 and ran for about five years — initially in their previous operators' liveries, which were red, albeit in shades different from that used by Highland.

The Royal Tigers were for operation to the ski slopes at Aviemore — services taken over from Smith of Grantown-on-Spey the previous year — and were rebuilt by coachbuilder Walter Alexander with a rack

Above: The Scottish Bus Group's first new Ford was this R192 with 45-seat Duple Midland body. It proved to be the first of many, Highland standardising on Fords from 1968 to 1980. *Harry Hay*

at the rear to hold skis. Achieved within the vehicles' overall 30ft length, this involved taking a short length out of the body and moving the rear bulkhead of the vehicle forward to leave an exposed external platform.

Assorted vehicles were still joining the Highland fleet from other SBG companies. These included 12-year-old Leyland Titan PD2s from Western and 12-month-old Albion Vikings from Central. There were even 20-year-old Tiger PS1s from Fife and Midland, although these were short-lived.

The company's last new AEC Reliance had entered service in 1962. In an echo of the Lowlander saga, Scottish Omnibuses had in 1966 purchased a batch of Reliance 590s which had proved troublesome, and three years later 16 of these made their way north.

In 1968 Highland received a record 16 new vehicles — or 17 if you include a Transit minibus. The 16 comprised six Bedford VAS, six Bedford VAM and four Ford R-series. Highland had a long tradition of Bedford operation, even if most of those added to its fleet were cascaded from other SBG fleets, and the 1968

vehicles were to be the last new Bedfords ordered.

In sharp contrast, Ford was about to become the company's main supplier, and by 1980, when the last were delivered, Highland would have taken delivery of over 150 R-series buses and coaches, making it one of Ford's biggest UK customers.

In 1970 came big changes. The Scottish Transport Group, which had a 50% share in the David MacBrayne bus, haulage and coastal-shipping business, took full control in 1969 and then set about rationalising MacBrayne's bus operations. There was a gradual transfer of MacBrayne's vehicles and services to other SBG companies, with most going to Highland.

First, in April 1970, were MacBrayne's Inverness-area services, quickly followed by services in Fort William and Kinlochleven. In September and October the services on Skye and in the Kyle of Lochalsh area, and in Oban and Ardrishaig were absorbed. The next parts of the MacBrayne business to be acquired were on Harris in the summer of 1971 and on Mull in November of that year. Finally, MacBrayne's Islay operations were taken over in January 1972.

This was massive expansion for Highland, involving around 120 MacBrayne vehicles and significant expansion of the company's operating territory southwards and westwards. One Bedford SB bus

Left: An ex-Ribble Leyland Royal Tiger shows the conversion work — carried out by Alexander at its Falkirk coachworks — which provided space for the carriage of skis at the back of the Leyland-built body. They operated in this form from 1968 to 1971. *Harry Ha*

Below: Central SMT's five unwanted Albion Vikings soon made their way north to Highland. Built as luxury coaches, these were among very few Scottish Bus Group Y-types not fitted with the standard roof-mounted destination display. New in 1966, they joined the Highland fleet the following year and were operated until 1981. One is seen leaving Elgin for Inverness in 1972. *Stewart J. Brown*

dered by MacBrayne was delivered new to Highland 1970. The company's last new Bedford, it survived til 1981, the year which marked the end of Bedford eration by Highland, the make having featured in the ghland Transport and Highland Omnibuses fleets for 9 years.

As part of the rationalisation of the MacBrayne usiness Highland also took over the Oban operations f Midland, along with 14 vehicles. Nine of these were eyland Tiger Cubs, a type not operated by Highland, nd in the interests of standardisation they were uickly exchanged for nine Reliances from the Midland eet.

With an enlarged fleet Highland adopted a new livery. There was some experimentation with a brighter red and cream, before the company settled on a striking combination of poppy red and peacock blue for its bus fleet in 1970. From 1976 a band of grey relief was added. Coaches retained the Happiways-inspired blue and grey scheme.

Highland was quick to withdraw some of the lightly-used MacBrayne services, and these were generally taken over by small operators or replaced by Post Bus services, which were expanding rapidly in Scotland in the early 1970s, typically run by nothing bigger than a Commer minibus. The Islay operations, for example,

Right: Most of the vehicles acquired from MacBrayne were Bedfords, including more than 30 VAS1 models with Duple-group bus bodies, as seen here outside the Highland office in Thurso in 1973.
Stewart J. Brown

Left: MacBrayne also operated AEC Reliances, and those which were specified as coaches received Highland's blue and grey coach livery. This 1962 Reliance had a 41-seat Duple Midland body.
Stewart J. Brown

were replaced by Post Buses 18 months after being taken over by Highland. The company also withdrew from Harris and Mull in the mid-1970s.

Highland had two depots in Inverness, one which had been used by Highland Transport and the other by Greig. These were replaced in 1972 by a new purpose-built depot and head office in Seafield Road. The head office had previously been at the town's bus station in Farraline Park.

While Fords dominated Highland's new-vehicle intake in the 1970s there were other types too. There were four new Leyland Leopards in 1973, bought specifically for long-distance services, then in 1978 the company took delivery of its first new double-deckers since the Highland Transport Guy Arab which had been an exhibit at the 1950 Commercial Motor Show. These were six Leyland Fleetlines with ECW bodywork. Nine more followed in 1979. They were not, however, Highland's first rear-engined double-deckers; these had been seven-year-old Alexander-bodied Fleetlines transferred from Fife in 1977.

Second-hand double-deckers in the 1970s included more Lowlanders, although by this time they were no longer in the first flush of youth as had been the ones with the original 1960s acquisitions. The last

Lowlanders for Highland, in 1976, were 13-year-old buses from Midland. One Lowlander came from outside the Group — a former Luton Corporation bus with East Lancs body which was acquired in 1974.

There were more interesting types too, such as two AEC Bridgemasters and an AEC Renown from Scottish Omnibuses, which Highland operated from 1973 to 1976. Other unusual purchases were six Leyland Titan PD3s from Edinburgh Corporation. These were 15 years old and joined the fleet in 1974, operating until 1976. They had forward-entrance Alexander bodywork. The operation of half-cab 'deckers by Highland ended in 1981, when the last Lowlander, a 1965 ex-Western bus, was withdrawn. However, as the last traditional front-engined double-deckers were departing a batch of 10 front-engined Ailsas was transferred from Fife, entering service in 1980.

Highland's last Fords entered service in 1980, along with its first heavyweight single-deck service buses, eight Leyland National 2s. Ten similar buses followed in 1981. All had gone by 1986, most being transferred to sister SBG company Kelvin Scottish in exchange for Leyland Leopards.

The Fords typically had a 10- or 11-year operating life with Highland, and as withdrawals started in the early 1980s their replacements were Leyland Leopards transferred from other Group companies. Most were only a year or two younger than the Fords they were replacing, but some were relatively modern vehicles, just three or four years old.

After the 15 Fleetlines in 1978/9 Highland received no more new double-deckers until 1983, when it took

Below: New to Edinburgh Corporation in 1957, this Leyland Titan PD3 was operated by Highland from 1974 to 1976. The unique bonnet assembly was designed to improve the driver's view of the kerb, which was restricted by Leyland's standard 'new-look' bonnet. Alexander built the body. *Harry Hay*

Left: Highland's first new rear-engined double-deckers were six Leyland Fleetline FE30AGR models delivered in 1978 in the relatively short-lived red, blue and grey livery. They had 75-seat ECW bodies.

Stewart J. Brown

delivery of six Leyland Olympians. By 1986 Highland would have 24 Olympians in service, all bought new. But odd second-hand double-deckers were acquired too, including two 10-year-old ex-London DMS-type Fleetlines in 1983 and five 11-year-old Leyland Atlanteans from Grampian Regional Transport in 1984.

The company's last new Leopards were delivered in 1982 and had 62-seat Alexander Y-type bus bodies; a Y-type Leopard bus normally seated 53, the extra nine seats being accommodated by using three-plus-two seating towards the rear. As with other Group companies, Highland then switched to Leyland's Tiger, which succeeded the Leopard. However, all of Highland's Tigers were coaches.

There was a further change of bus livery from 1980, the peacock blue being abandoned and the grey relief

introduced in the mid-1970s becoming the secondary colour. The end result was simpler but less striking. The coach livery changed in 1982, with the addition of white relief to the existing blue and grey.

The launch in 1983 of Scottish Citylink as a nationwide brand for the Group's long-distance coach services saw a number of Highland coaches receive the two-tone-blue and yellow Citylink colours.

There was a major reorganisation of the Scottish Bus Group in 1985 in preparation for local bus deregulation, but this had only a marginal effect on Highland, with the transfer back to Midland of the Oban depot and its operations, which had been added to Highland's territory in 1970. At the same time the company's name was changed to Highland Scottish Omnibuses, a style adopted for all SBG subsidiaries

Top: Newly arrived from Western SMT in September 1978, a Northern Counties-bodied Daimler Fleetline arrives at the Kessock Ferry terminus on what was then a busy Inverness town service. The Fleetline is crew-operated and carries a depot allocation plate, these being used briefly around this time after having been abandoned in the early 1960s. In the background work is getting underway on the new Kessock Bridge, which would see this service being massively reduced. *Stewart J. Brown*

Above: Highland's first Leyland Olympian is seen on an Inverness local service soon after delivery in 1984. Note the revised livery, with no blue relief but with an increased area of grey. Alexander built the lowheight body. *Stewart J. Brown*

and echoing the use of the fleetname Highland Scottish since 1979.

At the end of 1985 SBG took over the operations of Newton of Dingwall, a company which primarily ran express coach services and some school contracts, and as part of the deal Highland gained six Volvo coaches and four elderly double-deckers. This was a case of history repeating itself — Highland had 20 years earlier taken over a previous Newton business.

In January 1988, at which time Highland was running 160 buses, it was announced that SBG was to be privatised. Soon after the announcement Highland found itself facing competition on Inverness local services from a new operator, Inverness Traction, which was set up by a group of former Highland drivers and operated 12 second-hand Freight Rover Sherpas. After 12 months the struggling Inverness Traction was taken over by another small business which had started in 1988, Alexander North East, the Office of Fair Trading blaming the failure of Inverness Traction on unfair competition from Highland. However, Alexander North East was struggling too, and at the end of 1989 came a change in the ownership of Inverness Traction which was to have profound consequences for bus operations in and around Inverness: it was bought by Stagecoach. By this time it was running 30 vehicles.

Highland responded to Inverness Traction with its own minibuses, which included five new Renault S56s with Alexander bodywork, delivered in 1988. These were the last new buses for Highland under SBG ownership.

Despite having announced plans to privatise SBG at the start of 1988, it wasn't until three-and-a-half years later, in August 1991, that Highland was sold. Its fleet now numbered 141 vehicles, and its new owners were Clansman Travel (which owned Scottish Citylink) and Rapsons Coaches of Alness.

The new owners quickly announced plans to reduce the size of the business, and Stagecoach seized the opportunity to increase its recently established presence on local services in Inverness. By the end of 1991 Highland's fleet was reduced to 100 vehicles — around the number it had started with almost 40 years earlier.

Since the initial privatisation there have been changes in the structure and ownership of what was Highland Omnibuses, but in 2006 the entire operation is part of the Rapson Group, whose interests cover virtually all of the territory which Highland covered 20 years earlier, from Fort William in the south to Wick and Thurso in the north — and beyond, to Orkney.

Highland Omnibuses fleet profile

	1952	1966	1986
Fleet size	96	164	202
Average age (years)	8.9	9.9	8.1
Proportion of fleet over 10 years old	31%	44%	32%

Over the Backbone of England

DAVID WAYMAN looks back at his experiences as a part-time driver with Ribble in Manchester on trips across the Pennines.

"What, no driver for the half-past-three Bradford?" OK, the spare would have to take it.

On that Sunday, the last day of August 1975, the spare was the keen Ribble Motor Services part-time driver at Manchester depot who 30 years later would write about it for *Buses Yearbook*. He would need a guard (the local term for conductor), as the jointly operated Manchester–Bradford X12 limited-stop service was OMO, a 1970s acronym for one-man operation, and he wasn't then OMO-trained. Part-time Anwar Khokar was the spare guard.

Normally they worked on Ribble express or limited-stop services from Manchester to Blackpool, Morecambe, Keswick, or Penrith for Glasgow, and 'dupes' to Burnley or Clitheroe, all then crew-operated. Neither had ever covered a journey to Bradford. The problems were not over the route but the siting of some of the bus stops and the way into Bradford's Newton Street bus station. Oh, and they didn't have a timetable.

"Ah well," said the checker (inspector) at Chorlton Street coach station, "just keep going at a steady pace and turn left at the Craven Heifer in Bradford. If you're not sure of anything, ask the passengers."

With about twenty aboard No 1067 — one of the 'Lakeland Leopards' mentioned in *Buses Yearbook 2002* — they left on time at 15.30. In crew parlance 1067 was a bus, despite being numerically the first of five vehicles with Alexander Y-type 49-seat coach bodywork, new in 1969 and transferred to Ribble from North Western Road Car upon the reorganisation of some services in 1973. This included the takeover by Ribble of North Western's duties on the X12 and the transfer of some staff. Ribble repainted the vehicles into National Bus Company 'dual purpose' livery of white upper half and red lower, replacing the insipid all-white National coach garb. At that time Ribble shared garage premises in Manchester with North Western, which became part of National Travel (North West) from 1974, then National Travel (West) in 1977. Crews continued to call it North Western.

Power was ample with the Leyland O.680 11.1-litre engine. Except for some older examples with the part-synchromesh four-speed gearbox, Ribble's Leopards had the five-speed semi-automatic Pneumocyclic gearbox with full air change, adding to their versatility.

Versatility was certainly needed on that switchback course north-easterly to Bradford across the Pennines, England's backbone. Running alongside or intersecting with many Greater Manchester PTE routes, they at first

Left: Ribble Alexander-bodied Leopard 1070, 'The Boneshaker', shows the original style of front fitted to this batch of Y types.
David Wayman collection

On one of the services that nominally replaced the X12, a West Riding Alexander-bodied Leopard zooms along the Oldham internal by-pass on a wintry day, with the Mumps Bridge roundabout behind to the left. *David Wayman*

Left: **Leaving central Oldham on the A672 and almost at the 1,115ft Grains Bar summit, this Greater Manchester PTE Park Royal-bodied Leyland Titan is on the local service to Denshaw. The notable promontory behind is Besom Hill, visible from many miles away to the west.** *David Wayman*

climbed gently from Manchester city centre on Oldham Road, the A62, through drab inner suburbs with occasional glimpses of those moorland hills ahead.

After steeper climbing to the centre of Oldham they reached the coach station just off the A62 (8.4 miles, 28 minutes from start), where 1067's load doubled. From the nearby Mumps Bridge the bus climbed moderately at first, soon turning left from the A62 on to the much steeper A672, where the urban scene gradually gave way to dramatic vistas of hills and valleys ahead and left. Soon they reached 1,115ft at the bleak Grains Bar (11.6 miles), a rise of some 500ft within three miles. Then came a twisting 1.6-mile descent on a shelf of the steep-sided Upper Tame Valley to the operating limit of GMPTE, the picturesque

village of Denshaw (13.2 miles, 42min), with its crossroads just beyond the River Tame bridge.

Next there was the virtually straight 1.1-mile, 1-in-11 ascent of Sun Brow to that superb country hostelry, the Ram's Head. Now the bus was well out in the wilds and forging across Bleakedgate Moor before weaving up to the new Greater Manchester/West Yorkshire county boundary on the Pennine watershed (15.5 miles). With Moss Moor rising to the right, Windy Hill left and the Pennine Way crossing the A672, at 1,350ft it was the peak of the route, higher than the summits of Shap (1,036ft) and Beattock (1,029ft). In clear weather this stretch afforded Manchester-bound passengers a stunning panorama taking in the Peak District of Derbyshire and the distant Clwydian

Left: A regular on the X12 and here approaching Grains Bar from Bradford, West Riding Leopard 388 climbs out of the steeply sided Upper Tame Valley.
David Wayman

Right: At the end of its 1.1-mile slog at 1 in 11 from Denshaw while on a Mersey-Tyne journey, a Willowbrook-bodied Leopard in the Northern General fleet reaches the Ram's Head, another 1,100-ft location. Within two miles the coach will join the M62 eastbound.
David Wayman

Left: With 'Kamikaze' piloting and only days before the end of Ribble's X12 involvement, 1078 crosses the county boundary at the 1,350ft Windy Hill summit of the route. The M62 interchange is just down the hill behind the bus and the signpost points to the continuation of the Pennine Way.
David Wayman

untains in Wales. Often, however, rain would be shing down or visibility reduced to a few yards by fog. Now in Calderdale borough, 1067 zoomed downhill id under the M62 flyover, which at 1,221ft still mains the highest point on Britain's motorways. y the Spa Clough hairpin bend 1067 had descended me 400ft in just 1.8 miles. After more moderate ndulations alongside Booth Wood reservoir there ame a sharp descent to the happy little settlement of unning Corner (19.6 miles, 56min), the limit of West orkshire PTE operations.

There was easy cruising down through Rishworth to ipponden (21.7 miles, 62min) in the steep-sided yburn Valley, where the A672 ended as the A58 ropped in acutely and steeply from the left. With the ver below to the right 1067 went on through the amlets of Kebroyd and Triangle to the relatively busy

town of Sowerby Bridge (24 miles), the descent from the highest point having exceeded 1,000ft in just 8.4 miles.

Passengers were exchanged before the bus crossed the River Calder and then took a run at the winding, grinding 1.5-mile climb on grades of up to 1 in 8 to King Cross, followed by a drop of 350ft within the next 1.4 miles to Halifax town centre. At Halifax's Cross Field bus station (27.4 miles, 80min) Manchester-bound buses had to climb the parallel Great Albion Street then swing right over to the wrong side to perform a full-lock left-hand U-turn so as to reach the stand on the first platform, descending at 1 in 10. And steering was all muscle-powered!

After leaving Halifax centre the X12 went sharply upwards on the twisting A6036 through Northowram to a summit of 750ft at Shelf, near the Bradford city

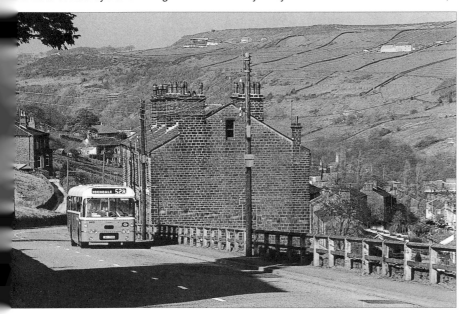

Left: The Ryburn Valley is another deep and steep-sided geological cut, joining the Calder Valley at Sowerby Bridge. Here a West Yorkshire PTE Plaxton-bodied short Leopard on the Halifax–Rochdale service leaves Ripponden by the A58, with which the A672 (route of the X12 and hidden to the bottom right of the picture) intersects acutely at the foot of the hill. *David Wayman*

Right: The need for a tight U-turn from Great Albion Street into the bus station at Halifax is demonstrated by a West Riding Leopard, Manchester-bound on the X12. *David Wayman*

boundary. The final four miles were easy, and the coach landed in Chester Street bus station (35.4 miles, 103min) just on the scheduled 17.13hrs. When the new Bradford Interchange came into use on 27 March 1977 the X12's time allowance between Halifax and Bradford was cut by three minutes both ways, although official mileage remained the same.

The return to Manchester with 1067 was uneventful, and at Chorlton Street an OMO driver had been found to do the 19.30 to Bradford and 21.30 return. The arriving 1067's chauffeur then had only to take a newish Leyland Atlantean, 1367, empty from Chorlton Street coach station to Manchester depot.

Sunday X12 journeys were every two hours from each terminus between 11.30 and 21.30. Monday to Friday there were additional scheduled journeys from Manchester at 07.30, 08.30, 09.30 and 16.30 and from Bradford at 06.30, 07.30, 09.30 and 16.30, but the final journey from each end was at 19.30. Saturday journeys from Manchester were at 06.35, then 07.30, and from Bradford at 06.30, both then hourly until 21.30. At that time Ribble's joint operating partner was the West Riding group. Each partner provided two vehicles for an hourly frequency and one for a two-hourly.

Wakefield based, the West Riding Automobile Co had been independent until acquisition by the state-owned Transport Holding Company in 1967. Then, following the formation of NBC in 1969, West Riding was incorporated, along with the Yorkshire Woollen District Transport Co of Dewsbury, into the new West Riding group. Vehicles on the X12 were from Woollen's Heckmondwike depot and usually bore the dual fleetname 'West Riding / Yorkshire', but Ribble staff simply used the 'Woollen' name.

Yes, and while 'bus' was used as a generic term, at times a more specific reference was required. A dual-purpose vehicle was a 'DP' (coach seats in a bus body, new 1965-8), while white coaches were known by the body name, such as 'Panorama' or 'Elite' or 'Dominant' all were Leyland Leopards and 49-seaters. Alexander bodied Leopards were simply 'Alexanders', while double-deckers were known by their chassis type. Eastern Coach Works-bodied Bristol RELH6Ls (all with superb brakes) were 'Bristols'. Manchester's allocation in 1975 comprised one Atlantean, two Bristols and 25 of the rest. In 1976 three DPs at Manchester were replaced by three new Dominants, two more being added later from elsewhere. Initially in National coach white, they were built to bus-grant specification and known as 'Dominant DPs'. Plaxtons and DPs had the 9.8-litre O.600 engine, and Alexanders, Bristols and all Dominants the 11.1-litre O.680.

A few weeks after his first foray Manchester depot's keen part-time driver was given a full Saturday duty on the X12 entailing the two 'lates', 15.30 and 19.30 from Manchester, 17.30 and 21.30 from Bradford, again with Alexander 1067. There being no other OMO-trained driver available, a guard had been rostered too. That guard failed to materialise, so two were found at short notice, one for each journey. The first lad had spent the morning checking X60 Blackpool duplicates, *i.e.* taking fares on the buses in the station so that they could go non-stop with driver only. He'd been busy, as it was the Illuminations season.

For the second X12 journey it was the famous and genial Ziggy. An OMO driver, he'd been to Bradford twice that day and would have exceeded his permitted hours by doing a third trip as a driver, but of course he

Left: **The bus with the musty smell: Bradford-bound Ribble DP 900 with Marshall body at the foot of Great Albion Street just after leaving Halifax bus station. Based on the Leopard PSU3/4 and earlier chassis, these DPs rode well, without the rolling characteristics of the later and softer-sprung PSU3B/4R-based Dominants.** *R. F. Mack*

Left: Dominant DP 1081, with roof-mounted destination display and non-standard fog lamps, poses at the entrance to Manchester depot before a Sunday duty on X12. *David Wayman*

could act as a guard. And how useful he was for pointing out such things as bus-stop signs hidden by overgrown foliage and which West Yorkshire PTE journeys should run ahead of the X12. Arrival time back in Manchester was 23.13 and depot finish 23.36.

Some time later Ziggy was driving the last X12 from Bradford. At Cunning Corner, a little early, he stopped to count some cash. A male passenger asked if there was time to dash across to the Cunning Corner Inn to use a facility. Yeah, OK. When Ziggy had finished counting he set off. At Manchester he discovered some property on the bus and realised that he'd suffered a memory lapse nearly 20 miles back. Ziggy looked over his shoulder for a while after that.

Ribble's longer-serving part-time OMO driver at Manchester, Stuart Mason, left in early 1976. The remaining part-timer was then given more X12 duties, usually the two late journeys, although he would not be OMO-trained until 1977 and therefore needed a guard. Often this would be the depot's veteran part-timer, Wilf Sidebottom. Quite a character was old Wilfie, having started his transport career with SHMD — the Stalybridge, Hyde, Mossley and Dukinfield Transport & Electricity Board (short and snappy title). He never liked the X12. Glasgows maybe, but when short-distance riders got on — at Ripponden for Sowerby Bridge, for instance — he would mutter: "Why can't they use their own flippin' local service?" It must have

reminded him of his long-gone days on t' Joint Board, as they called it.

David Mullineaux (pronounced 'Mully-no', please!) was another well-known part-time guard. His strident voice came in useful when directing crowds to the X60 or X70 at Blackpool. One wintry Sunday elsewhere, however, things went awry. David was paired with the usual part-time driver for the X12 'lates' with West Riding 386, an Alexander-bodied Leopard which Eric Rushworth had been given earlier as a changeover in Bradford for Ribble Dominant DP 1080. On the 19.30 from Manchester a male passenger of Middle Eastern origin appeared to ask David the fare to Bradford. But up on the dark and snowy moors the man became visibly agitated. David then discovered that he had in fact wanted Brierfield, north of Burnley on the X43 route, the stand for which was on the same platform as the X12 in Manchester. Luckily they hadn't passed the 'Woollen' partner but could see him approaching and flagged him down, sending the lost soul back.

With OMO training completed, doing the two late X12s on Saturday or Sunday (or occasionally both) became a regular though not exclusive pastime for Ribble's remaining part-time driver in the late 1970s. It was almost like a social club on wheels. One retired gent — well retired — would get on at Denshaw for Bradford at 16.12. "I've been travellin' over this route since North Western had petrol-engined Leyland Tigers on it!" he once stated. "Sometimes fog were so thick, bus had to crawl along over t' moors wi' t' guard sittin' out on t' nearside front wing, callin' to t' driver when he got too close to t' verge." He was missing for a few weeks and then returned. He'd been on a cycling trip — from Spain to Denmark.

Yes, and we'd have Harry and his lady companion waiting in Oldham at 19.58 on Saturdays, alighting at the Ram's Head and catching the same bus back at 22.30. Charlie and John would get on at Cunning Corner in the afternoon for Ripponden and Halifax respectively, returning on the last bus. Joyce, their neighbour and married to local Glenway Coaches senior driver, was an X12 regular too. So was Norma, who got on the last bus every Saturday at Halifax for Ripponden, on one occasion ecstatic after a big bingo win.

Now, when Alexander 1067 went into Ribble's Frenchwood central works at Preston, it came back with an Eaton two-speed rear axle (from a stick-change Leopard) locked in low ratio. This certainly made a difference to its acceleration, and it was clear that the engine had been 'opened up', for on the part-day X70 Manchester–Blackpool service 1067 could still easily reach the prevailing PSV motorway limit of 70mph — with the speedo needle on 90! (They always read fast in low axle-ratio.) Manchester's part-time pilot dubbed 1067 'The Screamer', for at full revs on those X12 banks it certainly announced its approach.

Its numerical neighbour, 1068, was less endearing. This he called 'The Rattler', for, while all five Alexanders may have qualified, 1068 was the worst. But it could move all right, and on a wet Sunday early in 1976 he and guard Johnny Tone, an old hand, had it on the 15.30 to Bradford. While the Alexanders' demisting equipment was poor, on 1068 it was pretty useless that day. Back in Manchester they asked for a changeover and got Dominant 1047, probably on its first-ever X12 journey, as Dominants were not then OMO-fitted. This had a fault too: on every left turn the w coolant' warning sounded falsely. But it was warm, d the windscreen clear. The driver subsequently rried a small bar of soap in his pocket — useful with paper towel for emergency demisting. Following a llision soon afterwards, 1068 came back with a front terior panel of the type intended for a rear-engined assis, such as the Bristol RE. This just didn't look ght. Some months later, it was changed for one of the iginal design, possibly from a North Western crapper'.

Regularly on arrival at Oldham of the Sunday 17.30 om Bradford, a middle-aged blonde-haired woman ith a young boy would be waiting for the eeds–Liverpool, due shortly after the X12. Despite Manchester' appearing on the blind she would outinely ask: "Diss duh Liverpool bus, luv?" With Rattler' 1068 she had an excuse, for the blind would lways slip during a journey and had usually passed Lowestoft', then 'London', and reached 'Liverpool'.

Those Alexanders covered tremendous mileage on he X12. 'The Flyer', 1069, also could accelerate lmost like a souped-up motor car. Ah yes, but it couldn't stop! Well, not on its nose, anyway, and as Graham Hutton trundled into the Donchaw dip one day Bradford-bound, a car pulled out at the crossroads. nevitably he walloped it, and 1069 finally stopped beyond the junction at the foot of Sun Brow. It then started to roll back, and there was nothing that Graham could do because the braking equipment had been damaged. A brake was eventually provided by the stone parapet of the Tame bridge, so 1069 had two ends damaged for the price of one. The replacement front panel was of a later type than the original, making 1069 easily distinguishable from the rest. Eventually all

five Alexanders were of different appearance from each other either at the front or the side, with variations in trim and position of other features.

Alexander 1070, 'The Boneshaker', was another to have its front exterior panel replaced following a collision. Subsequently, in place of its original one-piece windscreen, it acquired a split one complete with heating elements, regrettably not wired up to any switch. At about that time too 1070's engine became uncharacteristically rough, hence its nickname. It set Eddie Bibby's teeth on edge when he drove it, and he reckoned that the bearings must have assumed an oval shape. Yes, and it was pretty feeble. On the long drag up Sun Brow, for example, it would have to be dropped to second with a maximum speed of 18mph, losing time. The aged Continental cyclist could have overtaken it! So if it wouldn't go up the hills, by jings it had to go down 'em!

Oh, but 1071 was a complete contrast and known as 'The Sewing Machine'. That was Matt Caughey's description, and he loved driving it because of its nice, smooth, quiet engine, with plenty of oomph. The front panel, another replacement, had been fitted after 'Kamikaze' had grounded 1071 on a temporary Bailey bridge on service X48 to Sheffield. Subsequently a similar North Western machine rammed 1071 at the garage fuel pump, so it received a new rear end too.

One day the sole surviving part-timer had Dominant DP 1081 on the 15.30 to Bradford, but it had three faults, and on return he asked for a changeover. He got 'The Flyer', 1069, but it wasn't flying on that occasion. Progress uphill was decidedly sluggish, and the strong scent of fuel signalled heavy leakage. Arranged by phone from Halifax, the changeover was then changed

Right: 'The Flyer', 1069, outside its Manchester home and complete with revised front end following collision repairs.
David Wayman

over at Bradford. The only vehicle that Heckmondwike depot could send was 773, Yorkshire Woollen's cherished Roe-bodied Atlantean in 75th-anniversary traditional livery of maroon and cream with gold-leaf 'Yorkshire' fleetname. Tasteful!

Regarding changeovers, Ziggy brought one into Manchester one Sunday, calling: "You'll like this one, Dave!" He was right. It was 269, technically in the West Riding fleet, another Alexander-bodied Leopard. Like it? Ziggy's relief wanted to take it home! With 'opened-up' engine and splitter 'box, giving 10 ratios, it was the liveliest article he'd ever driven, romping up everything with ease. From a standing start at Stump Cross traffic lights he gave it full steam through all 10 ratios, and didn't it just zoom to the top, rear end lost in dust!

The winter of 1978/9 was a bad one for the X12. On Saturday 30 December the part-timer did the two

'lates' with 1068. Snow was blocking the A672 above Denshaw, so the route was diverted north of Oldham to Milnrow and then via the M62 to reach the A672 at Windy Hill. During the second weekend of January no services ran, due to the national fuel crisis. A week later snow again blocked the Pennine roads, stopping the X12 entirely. On Saturday 27 January, with cleared roads, the enthusiast-driver did the usual 'late' Bradfords, the first with Dominant 1026. It was leaking fuel, so back at Manchester he was given DP 917 as a changeover. Cold? Passengers getting off the old crate felt warmer in the Arctic wind.

He covered the same journeys the next day. It had snowed overnight throughout the region, and, adding to the woes, council workers in Calderdale had gone on strike, so there had been no road clearing or gritting over their 14-mile stretch from just below the M62

erchange to the Bradford boundary. Following a
...d-day rise the temperature then began to fall. Then
...b Adams came in from Bradford with Bristol 1020.
..., a rear-engined bus, light at the front end, on
...treated roads? Ah well, a changeover might have
...tailed loss of time, so Bob's relief set sail at 15.30.
...ristols had the semi-auto 'box with electric change.
...andled like precious china — for example,
...escending the steepest untreated banks at walking
...ace in crawler-first — 1020 behaved impeccably,
...ith hardly a hint of slip or slide anywhere. And it was
...nice warm bus.

The following day depot joker Reg Austen was on
...e 07.30 and took an Alexander down from Windy Hill
...t his usual pace, not knowing about the untreated
...ad until he started doing the Skater's Waltz. That he
...voided landing in the valley bottom must have been
...ttributable to his superb skills, or something.

There was more heavy snow on Sunday 4 February.
...Woollen did the first journey from Bradford at 11.30
...ut after returning cried off, leaving Ribble's intrepid
...part-timer by himself from 15.30 with Dominant DP
1078 on a four-hourly service until finish!

As for Bristols, one day 1017 behaved strangely on
X12, shooting forward when moving off routinely in
second. Well, it had just returned from a short
absence, and second gear position in the gate was
now linked to first ratio and *vice versa*. Modified driving
procedure was needed here — possible only due to a
fault in the speed-change baulking mechanism — with
appropriate remarks on the signing-off sheet later.

DPs 900 and 924 each spent some time allocated to
Manchester depot, but what a pair! 900 smelled musty
inside, while 924 was gutless for the X12 — saw a hill
and nearly fainted. On the 17.30 from Bradford one

dark and chilly evening, in the part-timer's hands it ran
a big end while climbing to Grains Bar. He eased it
over the top, then phoned for a changeover. The
Leeds–Liverpool soon came along and took 924's
passengers forward. Eventually Manchester depot
foreman Bill Dawson brought up Dominant DP 1079 to
deputise, having collected passengers waiting for the
19.30 from Manchester — without being able to take
their fares, of course; that had to be done out there at
high altitude. With Bill came a fitter driving a Leyland
National that had been summoned from Bolton to tow
924! And the part-time driver had missed his usual
refreshment.

Work at Manchester depot was diminishing, and by
1979 its 10 fine Dominants were being transferred
elsewhere. Many were undergoing conversion to OMO
and being repainted DP white/red, not necessarily at
the same time.

Ribble closed Manchester depot on Friday
7 November 1980. From the following day service X12
would be replaced partly by two Manchester–Leeds
services operated by the West Riding group. There are
no prizes for guessing who drove the last Ribble X12.
He had Dominant DP 1080, repainted in National
white, although all others of the same batch had gone
into DP livery. It wasn't the last bus scheduled into the
depot; that was the one on the X48 from Sheffield a
few minutes later. But 'Kamikaze' was on that and had
no intention of hanging about. 1080 was decorated for
the occasion and on a cold, wet and windy day left
Manchester on the 16.30 to Bradford, returning on the
19.30 and reaching Manchester coach station at 21.10;
after paying in it was back to the depot by 21.28 —
the last one. And that was that under the old order
for Ribble at Manchester.

**Right: The end of the X12
— or was it? Concerning
Ribble, yes; here a white-
liveried Duple Dominant
Leopard, having worked
the 16.30 from
Manchester on
7 November 1980, lays
over for 80 minutes at
Bradford Interchange
before the 19.30 return
journey. It is joined briefly
by a West Riding
National — another type
of bus used on the X12 —
which has just arrived
on the 17.30 from
Manchester. Posters in the
Dominant's windscreen —
courtesy of the author —
record the X12's imminent
demise.** *David Wayman*

The AECs of Nottingham City Transport

For the best part of 50 years, from 1929 to 1977, there were AECs in the Nottingham City Transport fleet. ROY MARSHALL tells the story.

All photographs by the autho[r]

Nottingham Corporation Tramways operated its first motor buses, double-deck Thornycrofts, between March 1906 and June 1908, when a variety of problems brought about their withdrawal. The war prevented further proposals being implemented, and it was not until 1920, under the ægis of J. Aldworth, that Dennis motor buses were introduced. Dennis supplied all NCT's new full-size buses until Mr Aldworth's retirement in 1928.

Early in 1929 W. G. Marks moved from Chesterfield Corporation to become General Manager of Nottingham. After an appraisal of the fleet he decided that a further 20 single-deck buses were needed, and so hired the requisite number of AEC Reliances with 30-seat bodywork by Short Bros. Shortly afterwards authorisation to purchase was given. Most were operated for 10 years.

Although most other makes of double-deck were on trial between 1929 and 1934, all prewar purchases were AECs — Regal single-deckers and Regent double-deckers. The first of these were 20 Regents ordered in 1929, all with English Electric 'camel'-roof bodywork featuring a distinctive hump above the gangway on the upper deck. Delivered in 1930, they were followed in 1931 by a further 50 Regents, all the original short-wheelbase model, with bodywork by Short, Park Royal and Brush. Five of the original 1930 batch had centre entrances.

All of the new deliveries were to replace obsolete Dennis models, improve services and serve new council housing estates. However, such was the progress in the development of vehicles that all of the 1930 vehicles would be replaced by 1939, some finding further service with other operators.

In 1932 NCT had on extended loan a longer-wheelbase version of the Regent, and this resulted in an order for eight, with 56-seat Park Royal bodywork. Shortly after delivery one had its body removed and

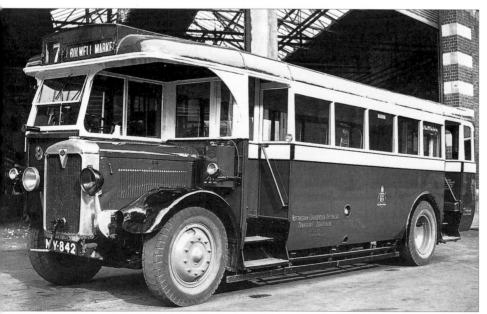

Left: One of Nottingham's first AEC Reliances with Short Bros bodywork, initially hired but subsequently purchased.

Right: The distinctive English Electric 'camel roof' on the 1929 batch of AEC Regents.

Left: Eight longer-wheelbase AEC Regents with Park Royal bodywork were delivered in 1932. Those that survived in service postwar were considered good enough to be converted to 7.7-litre diesel engines in 1947.

chassis converted for the fitment of a tower-wagon body, to maintain overhead wires for the undertaking's trams. A new chassis for the spare body arrived in 1933.

Following a quiet period during the worst years of the Depression the Corporation embarked on a massive tram-to-trolleybus conversion. However, the appointment of another new General Manager, J. L. Gunn, brought about a change in policy in the shape of orders for AEC Regents with 8.8-litre oil engines, crash gearboxes and metal-framed bodywork by

Metro-Cammell or Northern Counties. In all, 57 were delivered between 1934 and 1936.

Later in 1936 a further change took place when the newer 7.7-litre engine was adopted, coupled to a pre-selector gearbox. Some of the first of these buses — there were 121 delivered by 1939 — replaced the last tramcars in 1936. Bodywork was by Metro-Cammell and Cravens. These were first-class buses which gave excellent service throughout the war years — apart from those with Cravens bodywork, which were delivered in 1937 after acceptance of the lowest tender

Left: Metro-Cammell-bodied AEC Regent in Trinity Square.

Right: Pre-selector gearboxes characterised 121 AEC Regents built just prior to the outbreak of World War 2.

and which would require extensive rebuilding postwar.

Also in 1937 came five Cravens-bodied Regals, which were required for two services. They had rear-entrance bodywork with dual-purpose seating for 32. Two of these vehicles were requisitioned for war service.

Increased peak-hour requirements in the early postwar years, along with delays in the delivery of new buses, saw NCT buying second-hand Regents in 1947 and 1948, four coming from neighbouring West Bridgford and 11 from Halifax. Most had oil engines, although some of the Halifax buses and the

four from West Bridgford were petrol-engined.

The postwar equivalent of NCT's 1938/9 Regents — 30 Regent IIIs with 56-seat Metro-Cammell bodywork — arrived in 1949, somewhat later than planned. To obtain further new vehicles an order was placed for 41 Regents with bodywork by Charles Roberts of Wakefield to the new 8ft maximum width. These entered service in 1949/50.

There was a return to AEC single-deckers in 1951 with the delivery of three East Lancs-bodied Regal IIIs to replace the three surviving 1937 Regals. Once again they had rear-entrance bodywork, this time by East

Right: Five Cravens-bodied AEC Regals were delivered in 1937 with dual-purpose seating.

Lancs. These were NCT's first East Lancs bodies and were ordered when the undertaking's traditional suppliers declined to quote for building such a small batch of buses.

The final Regent IIIs were 80 delivered in 1953/4. The first 70 had 56-seat metal-framed highbridge Park Royal bodywork, but the specification of the last 10 was changed; these had 53-seat lowbridge bodywork, still by Park Royal, but of composite construction, and these buses replaced wartime Daimlers on the rapidly-expanding services to Clifton Estate.

Nottingham's final Regents were 65 Mark V models, albeit still with exposed radiators, which entered service in 1955/6. They had 61-seat Park Royal bodies and synchromesh gearboxes and replaced prewar Regents and wartime utilities.

Left: NCT purchased second-hand AEC Regents in 1947/8. This was one of four acquired from West Bridgford.

Left: Another source of second-hand Regents for NCT in the immediate postwar years was Halifax Corporation.

Left: It was not until 1949 that NCT took delivery of its first new postwar buses, numbering 30 Metro-Cammell-bodied AEC Regent IIIs.

For a time it appeared that the Regent Vs would be NCT's last AECs, after almost three decades in which the Southall manufacturer had been the undertaking's principal supplier. A change of policy which saw the specification of buses with synchromesh gearboxes allowed Leyland to quote for Titan PD2s, and it was Titans which were delivered in 1958/9, no doubt to Leyland's delight and AEC's chagrin. But the introduction of rear-engined models brought further

changes in policy, and in addition to Leyland Atlanteans and Daimler Fleetlines, NCT took delivery of 42 AEC Renowns for uses that included some of the more lightly trafficked former trolleybus routes. The body order was divided between Weymann, which bodied 35, and Northern Counties. All were 70-seaters.

In September 1968 came a major influx of AECs, albeit second-hand, when NCT took over the bus

Right: NCT took early advantage of the new 8ft width limit with an order for 31 Roberts-bodied AEC Regents.

Below: In 1951 NCT ordered its first East Lancs bodies on three AEC Regal IIs, to replace the 1937 Regals.

operations of West Bridgford UDC. This fleet of 28 had been 100% AEC, ranging from 1947 Regent IIs to 1967 Swifts.

The very last AECs for Nottingham, delivered in 1969, were six Swift 505s with 43-seat dual-door bodywork by Northern Counties. However, unlike most of their illustrious predecessors, the Swifts were short-lived, lasting only six years before being sold to Grimsby-Cleethorpes Transport.

Operation of AEC Regents, which had started in 1930, ended in 1976, when the last of the Mark Vs were withdrawn. And AEC operation ceased altogether the following year, with the withdrawal of the last of the Renowns, severing a link which had endured for nearly half a century.

Shocks, Surprises and the Out-of- the-ordinary

STUART JONES, editor of industry magazine *Bus & Coach Buyer*, takes time off to travel down memory lane.

"I'd like a nice surprise," my mother would say when I, devoid of inspiration, would ask what she wanted for Christmas or her birthday. The fact that, at the time, my pocket money was two old shillings a week rather limited the chances of my creating a 'wow' factor, but perhaps her approach contributed to my liking for the unexpected, the out-of-the-ordinary and the downright odd.

As with so many things in my life, an interest in buses came relatively late; I was 11 before it really got me, though there had been nudges in that direction before. Every school day meant two five-mile journeys

on Midland Red's 144 service. I only did the bit between Rubery and Bromsgrove on a route that then ran from the gloomy depths of the company's Birmingham bus station to Worcester and beyond to Malvern. It wasn't the use of BMMO-built D9 double-deckers that would make me take note (they were the usual fodder); it was the arrival of the example that had the platform and stairwell painted in a ludicrous multi-speckled manner or of one of the all-over

Below: Midland Red's attractive D9 was the standard vehicle on the author's trips to school. An immaculate preserved example recalls the great days of Britain's biggest bus operator outside London. *David Cole*

advertisement buses. Most memorable among the latter was the Hall Green Stadium example in green and white, exhorting potential punters to go to the dogs on 'Mondays, Wednesdays and Saturdays at 7.30pm'. More recently I've been amazed that Corgi managed to justify producing not just the C5 coach in model form but also the D9 in a wealth of different variants, including the Hall Green example.

What generates that *frisson* of excitement in one's encounter with a bus is hard to define. When I was a kid, one that I hadn't seen before that I could underline in my Midland Red fleet list was enough to do the trick, though as the years went by these occasions became rarer and usually required travelling further afield — to such exotic spots as Leicester or Stafford — until I gave up noting the numbers altogether.

The first of a new type would do it too, possibly preceded by a telephone call from one of my bus mates who had already seen it. Plaxton Supreme-bodied Leyland Leopards in the poppy-red and white 'local coach' livery, replacing the CM6 coaches on the Birmingham–Worcester express services, were a case in point, though the idea that a Plaxton-bodied Leopard was once something special seems somewhat strange now. Surely I should have been mourning the passing of Midland Red's last in-house coach design. The Worcester CM6s were different from the rest of the 30 built in not having toilets, whereas those working down the M1 were CM6Ts; 'T' for toilet — simple really.

A few years later some friends bought a CM6T after it had served with a contractor. I believe it may also have worked with Morris of Pencoed, as it carried a blue and white livery, and Morris also ran a number of other BMMO-built buses at the time. Wonder what kind of a welcome they got in the hillsides? Anyway, we converted it into a caravan, complete with bunk beds, tables and a servery, and twice went to Amsterdam in it. The first trip also took in Utrecht, where we parked in the bus station among the Dutch-bodied Leylands, while the second was memorable for the minus-double-figure temperatures experienced; the diesel froze in the fuel lines, forcing us to rig a temporary fuel tank in the saloon in order to keep it running — once we finally managed to get it going in the first place!

I was also fascinated by the arrival in 1970 of Midland Red's Plaxton Derwent-bodied Ford R192s, designated the S25 class by the powers that be in Edgbaston. Set off with a cream band on their red paintwork and a dreadful green colour applied to much of the interior, they were so different and modern in appearance compared with the frumpy BMMO S14-S17 family with which I was familiar. To begin with none was allocated near my home in Bromsgrove, so Hereford and Ludlow had to be visited. Predictably, my favourite among a Ford fleet that grew to be quite large was the oddball example, XUX 417K, similar in appearance to Midland Red's own but acquired with the business of Coopers of Oakengates, Shropshire. Years later a sad-looking example found in the yard of Bartons of Maynooth in Ireland was one of those pleasant surprises, just because I was glad to see an old acquaintance still around. The real surprises among Midland Red's Ford/Derwents were those cut down by the company to make 27-seat midibuses. With their short rear overhangs they became known to us as 'Stumpies'. Midland Red West was later to refurbish two of them as 23-seater coaches for private-hire duties, giving them the white coaching livery to boot! They had tables too, which presumably made them 'executive' coaches, though the retention of a full destination display hardly fitted that image.

Visits to depots would often turn up something unusual, nothing more so than the one and only UK-registered Scania CR145 integral coach, HOM 682L, which I encountered at Digbeth Coach Station. It was on demonstration at the time. I thought it an amazing beast, though hardly good-looking, its slab sides contrasting with the CM6Ts then still plying to and from London. Soon afterwards I saw that other oddity, NBC's solitary Alexander M-type Leopard, which, like the Scania and virtually every other coach in the place, sported National white.

Liveries can shock you too, like the first time one of the Standerwick Bristol VRL/ECWs hove into view in white rather than cream and maroon — it wasn't an improvement! National white didn't suit most older coaches, so it might have been nice to see one of the Worcester CM6s in the poppy-red and white 'local coach' livery, but, as far as I am aware, it never happened. One bus that did get it — indeed, one class of buses — was Trent's 1962 batch of Alexander-bodied Leyland Tiger Cubs. These were very bussy-looking dual-purpose 41-seaters, even when new, and by the time I saw YRC 183 in Matlock in the mid-1970s red paint over the side flashes denuded them of

Below: With its multitude of small windows the BMMO S17 was perhaps robust-looking rather than attractive. This preserved bus, with bodywork completed by Willowbrook, is seen outside the Kidderminster station of the Severn Valley Railway. David Cole

Above: A pair of Midland Red's Plaxton-bodied Ford buses stand outside the company's Telford depot — now part of the Arriva empire. *David Cole*

whatever external 'coachiness' they ever possessed. I don't blame NBC subsidiaries for applying the style wherever they could in preference to unrelieved red or green, perhaps my favourite application being the blue and white carried for a short while by East Yorkshire's Plaxton Elite-bodied Leopards.

We mis-spend our youth in numerous ways, one of my favourites being day trips by car to visit the more interesting operators in a remote area. I'd regularly stay with a friend in Northampton, and we'd set off from there in whatever direction took our fancy. One morning — I think it was a Sunday — Northampton was enveloped in freezing fog that suggested even poorer results than usual from my Kodak Instamatic. Looking out of the window of Malcolm's flat in Lings, we were more than a little concerned to see Northampton Transport 247, one of the undertaking's many Roe-bodied Daimler CVG6s, slide gracefully down the hill, over a T junction and come to rest against the kerb opposite. Rushing downstairs with the camera got me a reasonable shot of the bus, apparently unscathed, recovering its dignity and about to pull back onto the correct side of the road to continue its journey.

One Saturday morning, possibly on the day previous to the CVG6 incident, we were on our way into Burton-upon-Trent when we found our way blocked by two double-deckers that had collided on a bend. Accidents involving two buses travelling in opposite directions are unusual enough, but this one was particularly noteworthy in that it involved two vehicles from different municipal fleets, both of which were early Leyland Atlanteans that had been acquired secondhand. In the (two-tone) blue corner in this apparently evenly

matched contest was Derby 61 (UBX 48), a 1960 Weymann lowbridge example that had been new as one of a batch of five to BET subsidiary James of Ammanford; it had passed to South Wales Transport two years later and served City of Oxford Motor Services for some years before reaching Derby in 1976, along with some other Atlanteans that had enjoyed the same list of owners. In the red (,white and green) corner was East Staffordshire 2 (222 BTP), a Metro-Cammell-bodied PDR1/1 of 1963 that had been new to Portsmouth, arriving in Burton in 1975. This had been working the 7 service to Manners Estate, while the Derby bus was on the 103 Derby–Burton route. The front offside corners had come into contact on a bend that my pictures suggest the Derby bus may have been taking too widely, narrowly avoiding pushing the East Staffs bus into a lamp-post. The drivers'-side windows had finished up, unbroken, inside each other, but the damage sustained by both buses was sufficiently extensive to ensure that they had carried their last passengers; neither would appear in the next edition of the appropriate Fleetbook. After a brief visit to Burton bus station, where Massey-bodied Daimler CCG5s, Willowbrook-bodied Fleetlines and East Lancs Dennis Dominators were the order of the day, we walked back to the car and saw the unlucky No 2 being towed away.

Trips to Wales were always exciting. If you got up early you could be wandering around Newport,

Above: The one and only UK Scania CR145 was a demonstrator which was operated by Midland Red. It is seen here prior to entering service in July 1973. *Stewart J. Brown*

Below: Overall National white was not an improvement on the dark red and cream originally applied to Standerwick's impressive Bristol VRL coaches. One pauses in Coventry on its way from London to Southport in 1973. *Stewart J. Brown*

surrounded by Metro-Scanias that were the epitome of modernity, at the time when the bell for morning school would normally have been ringing. The pleasant surprises were the AEC Regent Vs, when you could find them, which you could with East Lancs bodywork in Cardiff, with Massey bodywork with Rhymney Valley/Bedwas & Machen, with Metro-Cammell, Willowbrook, Weymann and Longwell Green bodywork with Taff Ely and with Park Royal, Willowbrook and Weymann bodywork running around Swansea with South Wales Transport. My favourite SWT AECs were the ex-Western Welsh Renowns with Northern Counties bodywork.

At the time of my one and only visit to the Gelligaer depot Rhymney Valley had not long since absorbed the Gelligaer, Caerphilly and Bedwas & Machen fleets. Some of the buses around the yard and lined up on the road outside were still in the colours of their previous owners, but for once I preferred the new scheme of rich brown, yellow and cream, which looked great on Bristol VRs and half-cabs alike. There haven't been many other new liveries since that which have

Above: Ouch! Two Atlanteans come to an untimely end near Burton-upon-Trent — a Derby bus on the left, and an East Staffordshire vehicle on the right. *Stuart Jones*

Below: The East Staffordshire Atlantean heads back to the depot for the last time. *Stuart Jones*

Above: East Lancs-bodied Dennis Dominators were the standard choice at East Staffordshire.
David Cole

Below: In the mid-1970s Cardiff was still operating Guy Arabs, including a large batch with Alexander bodywork which entered service in 1966.
Stewart J. Brown

Above: Just two years after buying conservative Guy Arabs Cardiff was adding dual-door standee AEC Swifts to its fleet. There were 20, with Alexander bodywork accommodating 63 passengers — 16 of whom had to stand.
Stewart J. Brown

been an improvement on what went before, though it was fabulous to see Grey-Green's Alexander-bodied Volvo B10Ms running through Central London on the 24 in something other than red. Alongside all those anonymous bullseye-branded buses they shouted: 'Here comes the new order!'

Returning to the subjects of Massey bodies, liveries, Staffordshire and Wales, there was the time I was visiting Stevensons of Uttoxeter —well, Spath actually — to interview Managing Director Julian Peddle. I was used to the yellow, black and white colours and the fact that virtually anything from a Routemaster to brand-new Bristol VRs could appear in them, but what I wasn't prepared for was the blue Bedwas & Machen livery adorning PAX 466F, the 1968 Massey-bodied Leyland PD3/4 that had started off as the tiny Welsh municipality's No 6. It looked immaculate in the sunshine, but it wasn't long before it lost the blue in favour of yellow. Julian, until early 2006 the owner of MK Metro, still has it; when I interviewed him again in 2005, there it was in the corner of the yard at Milton Keynes, more than twice its age when I first encountered it.

Both my mother and father were from families with six children, so I had plenty of aunts and uncles to visit. Sometimes this created spotting opportunities. Uncle Mike and Aunty Pam lived at Alton in Hampshire; they still do. A walk from their house would take me past the small Alder Valley depot, where on

the forecourt I once saw an ex-Southdown Bristol RESL/Marshall — a turn-up, as at the time I didn't know the company had any. A few years earlier I might have seen those bonneted Dennis Falcon P5s in two greens and cream that I've always thought were lovely-looking buses, but no — they'd long gone.

More interesting still than the old Aldershot & District premises was the large yard of Warren's, better known as Altonian Coaches. On my first visit, to my absolute amazement, there was the Scottish Aviation-bodied Tilling-Stevens half-cab that I had seen in the pages of my Blandford *British Buses and Trolleybuses since 1945* — one of the first books in my now quite large bus library. Not only was it still there in its faded orange and cream; it was still running, with another similar bus withdrawn in the yard. The runner was later sold to Classic Coaches of Wombourne, where I got to travel on it. It's still around; most recently I saw it in green and yellow livery with Wulfrunian fleetname.

Altonian had a few other surprises among its fleet, including a former Grey-Green Bedford VAM with a peaked roof box that wouldn't have looked out of place

Above: In the early 1970s Metro-Scanias were the epitome of modernity. Newport was not the only South Wales operator of the type; this was one of three operated by Taff Ely. Note the ornate fleet-number transfer. *Stewart J. Brown*

Right: AEC Regent Vs were popular in South Wales. This 1966 bus is seen in Pontypridd in 1974. Operated by Western Welsh, it had a 65-seat Northern Counties body. *Stewart J. Brown*

on a Silver Star Harrington. There's an article to be written on the cameo appearances of buses and coaches in films; does anyone else recall seeing an Altonian Bedford VAL in a 'St Trinian's' film that also featured the Longmoor Military Railway?

I didn't have to go far from home to see something out of the ordinary. A first sighting of a new purchase by one of the local independents was always something special, especially if its arrival had not been heralded in advance. The Kilometregobbler was just such a coach. I'd noticed it driving through Bromsgrove one day with its title on the glass panel beneath the rear window and didn't know what it was. Only later did it transpire that it had been bought by Harris of Catshill, who traded as Harris Silver Queens. Later still I identified it as a Jonckheere Solaire-bodied AEC Reliance 760. It had previously been with The King's Ferry, where owner Peter O'Neill had come up with the name. OK, so when I first saw it I thought it was probably an UTIC-AEC, but it was an easy mistake to make.

The Solaire wasn't exactly the most common coach in the UK, the only other one I saw being Mid Warwickshire Motors' example, also on AEC chassis, which I encountered in Coventry's Pool Meadow bus station. In 1977 I went to the Le Mans 24 Hours in the Gobbler, as it became known, with my friend Charlie at the wheel. Quite a number of us slept in the luggage boot, which, with the cars screaming round the track all night, was the quietest place we could find. The funny thing about the Gobbler — and something I didn't

realise for some years — was that the front grille was mounted the wrong way up, so that the 'J' (for Jonckheere) looked like a 'C' with a bit chopped off. It's still my favourite coach to have been operated by Harris's, though for sheer surprise value and spotting pedigree the relatively brief stay of the Red Baron has to be mentioned. In a fleet painted yellow and white — most bought new, with registrations in multiples of the same number — she was not distinguished with a royal title such as Queen Elizabeth. No; for reasons I never fathomed this 1965 ex-Barton AEC Reliance/Harrington Grenadier was painted bright red and named after a German fighter ace … or was it Snoopy's alter ego? What a classic!

Not too far distant from home was the Black Country. On a number of occasions I'd been to the main depot of Watts of Lye, which operator later became a bit more ambitious, using the title 'Watts of the West Midlands'. I'd often see its buses carrying workers to the Austin plant at Longbridge, sometimes still in the

Above: One of the attractions of South Wales in the 1970s was the number of small municipal fleets. Merthyr Tydfil operated this East Lancs-bodied Leyland Leopard, one of six delivered in 1968.
Stewart J. Brown

Below: Rhymney Valley District Council had not long been in existence when the author visited South Wales. The operator's unusual but attractive livery is seen on this Massey-bodied AEC Regent V.
Stewart J. Brown

Above: A surprise for the author was finding this Leyland Titan PD3 in the yard at Stevensons of Uttoxeter. It had a side-gangway lowbridge body — the last bus built to this layout — by Massey. Delivered to Bedwas & Machen Urban District Council in 1968, it is seen here in that operator's depot in 1974, just after the creation of Rhymney Valley District Council. *Stewart J. Brown*

Below: An unusual coach which the author has encountered on a number of occasions is this Tilling-Stevens with Scottish Aviation body, which spent some time with Classic Coaches of Wombourne. *David Cole*

Above: The very rare AEC Reliance with Jonckheere Solaire body, in service with Harris Coaches of Catshill. *David Cole*

full livery of their previous owners. One such I recall was a Western SMT Leopard/Y type. What came as a splendid surprise to me was finding Watts' second yard, full to the brim with withdrawn vehicles, many of them relatively exotic, including at least seven of those ex-Standerwick VRLs. They were all looking a bit past it in the colours of Thomas Cook and ICL (International Coach Lines), but hey — seven of them, and on my doorstep. There was an ex-North Western Dennis Loline too, still in the Crosville green it had acquired when North Western was broken up.

Back in the days before EFE sponsorship, when the Showbus rally took place alongside Hillingdon Show and my younger sister would happily come along so she could have a go on the dry ski slope, there were rows of London RTs relieved by the odd RTL, RTW or RLH. Impressive how I can remember all those codes, isn't it? How many London enthusiasts could have successfully identified the differences between a Midland Red D5, D7, D9 or D10?

But I digress. The fact is that all those venerable AECs (and Leylands) didn't interest me much: there were too many of them, they all looked much the same, and to me they were ... well, slightly boring. No, I wanted something a bit more off-the-wall, a bit racy — like GRX 1N, Reading's first MCW Metropolitan

double decker, all gleaming and new. It looked the bee's knees then, and I appreciated it. I doubt that any other from the batch would still have any *cachet* with me, but were I to come across that one ... well, it would be a welcome experience, like being reunited with an old friend.

Nowadays I'm rarely startled by what I see, as I've invariably read or written about new vehicles in advance of encountering them, but every now and again it does happen, and something totally unexpected creeps up on me unawares.

One manufacturer has done it to me twice now — Neoplan. There I was at the 1996 IAA German Commercial Motor Show when I turned a corner and saw it. Surely not, but, yes, the Starliner was for real. Then, at the 2004 IAA, it happened again; NeoMAN had brought out another one that was even more outrageous in its futuristic appearance. I'm sure I wasn't the only one stunned by that one, and I received a second stunning when I got inside and saw the fabulous way that the panoramic windows had been used to make the interior so light. Even better than a Harrington Cavalier — yes, even one of Southdown's, with 2+1 seating.

When I started this I was going to finish by telling you of the almost unbelievable bus sights that I have seen in China and India in recent years, but a check on the word count tells me I've already exceeded what the editor asked for.

You'll not be surprised that I don't approve of upsetting editors.

Change on Clydeside

In the mid-1990s Clydeside 2000, formerly part of the Scottish Bus Group, was in the throes of change. BILLY NICOL illustrates the changing face of the Clydeside fleet.

Left: Clydeside 2000 received its first Leyland Nationals in May 1993, when it acquired the business of Inverclyde Transport of Greenock. This one-time Hants & Dorset bus is seen in Greenock town centre soon after being repainted in Clydeside colours. All of the Nationals had gone by the end of the year, by which time Inverclyde had recommenced services in competition with Clydeside.

Right: In 1993 Clydeside 2000 acquired a number of Leyland Leopards to replace double-deckers. This Plaxton-bodied example was acquired from East Midland but had been new to London Country. It is seen in Paisley, with a Strathclyde Buses MCW Metrorider behind.

Right: Seen in central Paisley in an experimental livery with more red than normal is a Clydeside 2000 Fleetline with Alexander body, one of the few double-deckers in the fleet in 1993. It was decided not to proceed with this livery layout.

Left: Clydeside 2000 operated a small number of Dennis Dominators and replaced them while they were still relatively young with second-hand Leopards. The latter included examples from Lancaster City Transport, one of which, still in Lancaster's blue and off-white livery, is seen in Glasgow. The Alexander Y-type body was, of course, a familiar type in the Clydeside fleet, although those built for Lancaster were easily identifiable by features such as the use of opening sections on all of the side windows.

Right: The most common type of minibus in the Clydeside 2000 fleet was the Alexander-bodied Dodge S56, a type purchased in large numbers by the Scottish Bus Group. A 1987 example waits at Paisley Cross in 1994.

Above: Clydeside 2000 received its first new full-size vehicles in the summer of 1994. These were seven Volvo B6s with Alexander Dash bodywork, some of which, like this bus seen in Paisley, entered service in overall white.

Below: Ownership of Clydeside 2000 passed to British Bus in 1994, and its new owners were quick to invest in new buses. These included Scania N113s with East Lancs MaxCi bodywork, which were among the first low-floor buses in Scotland.

Right: Other new buses — all purchased from dealer stock — were four Scania L113s with Alexander Strider bodywork. One loads in Glasgow *en route* to Erskine, with a Strathclyde Buses Atlantean in the background.

Left: Also added to the fleet in the British Bus buying spree were 10 Dennis Lances with Plaxton Verde bodywork. British Bus introduced a bigger Clydeside fleetname, dropped the '2000' and introduced a brighter livery of red, white and yellow.

Right: Seen outside Glasgow City Chambers in 1995 is one of a pair of Dennis Darts with Plaxton Pointer bodywork delivered that year. It is operating on the Scottish Citylink service to Glasgow Airport.